Sidney Gilpin

The Songs and Ballads of Cumberland and the Lake Country

With Biographical Sketches, Notes, and Glossary. Second Series

Sidney Gilpin

The Songs and Ballads of Cumberland and the Lake Country
With Biographical Sketches, Notes, and Glossary. Second Series

ISBN/EAN: 9783744777490

Printed in Europe, USA, Canada, Australia, Japan

Cover: Foto ©Thomas Meinert / pixelio.de

More available books at **www.hansebooks.com**

THE

SONGS AND BALLADS

OF

CUMBERLAND

AND THE LAKE COUNTRY,

WITH

BIOGRAPHICAL SKETCHES, NOTES,
AND GLOSSARY.

By SIDNEY GILPIN.

SECOND SERIES.

And at request would sing
Old songs, the product of his native hills.
WORDSWORTH.

SECOND EDITION.

CONTENTS.

Portrait of ROBERT ANDERSON, engraved from an original painting by George Sheffield.

MARK LONSDALE.

vi.

vii.

MARK LONSDALE.

ARK LONSDALE was born in Caldew-gate, Carlisle, on the 26th of May, 1758, in an old-fashioned cottage which is now razed to the ground, but which, with the garden, occupied the site of the present Ragged Schools. He was the eldest son of John Lonsdale of Caldewgate, blacksmith, and Isabella Mark, his wife, who formerly belonged to Thurstonfield. Of his early education very little is known, but there is not much doubt it was of a common order, as he was sent at an early age to follow the business of a pattern designer. As he grew up to manhood, not being satisfied with the drudgery attending his calling, and finding Carlisle too limited for the full scope of his ambition, he, like many others, made his way towards the metropolis, where there is a wider field for competition, and where merit has a better chance of success. He had not been long in London before he turned his pursuits, both as author and mechanic, to the most intricate parts of theatrical amusement. His success in this soon procured his promotion as manager of Sadler's Wells, which post he held for a number of years. He was the immediate predecessor of Charles Dibdin the younger. When he gave up his situation at Sadler's Wells he became part proprietor of the magnificent pictures, the Battle of Seringapatam, &c., which were exhibited at the Lyceum. It was here that Mark Lonsdale projected that elegant and instructive scenic exhibition and oral description denominated ÆGYPTIANA, an exhibition which at once demonstrated that though he had not had the benefit of a classical education, he was not wanting in a knowledge of the classics. This exhibition, although a convincing proof of his abilities, was an utter failure in a pecuniary point of view. It was his intention, had his first plan succeeded, to have given the peculiarities of geography, natural history, and manners of the inhabitants of other countries, but a disarrangement of his circumstances was the reward of his first praise worthy endeavour.

He then retired to Ireland, where he was engaged in tuition, and became tutor to a young nobleman. The following letter to his niece, Miss Isabella Lonsdale, (afterwards Mrs. Joseph Railton,) gives an interesting sketch of his manner of life in Ireland.

TULLAMORE, 16*th Dec.*, 1810.

I am still going on very successfully in my tuitions, but, in consequence of short days and bad weather, am obliged to contract my circle into a narrower compass. My principal station is now in the town I write from, a very bustling, dirty, genteel, uncomfortable place, about six miles from

Clara. Here I am well employed for three weeks in the month, and the fourth week I spend in Maryborough, the principal town in the adjoining county, and about the size of Caldewgate. The distance is eighteen Irish miles, (about twenty-three English,) and I walk it on a Sunday, let the weather be fair or foul, equipt in the common foul weather dress of the country, viz: tann'd leather leggings, a frize great coat, an oak shillela, and a glazed hat,—such is the costume of an Irish traveller, and such a figure may very likely be presented to you in Scotch Street, some day or other within the course of the next summer. . . . The gentry are, one and all, very bad paymasters,—and one had need have the patience of Job to get an account settled with them ; all my connexions, however, are very safe I believe, though rather slow. I have no fear of losing anything in the end,— and one or two of them being exceptions to the general rule, supply me with cash enough to go on with.

In my last, I think, I gave you a sketch of my usual engage-ments for the summer ; and it may perhaps interest or amuse you to know how I am employed for one day in Tulla-more. At eight o'clock I attend at Mr. Killaly's, (the engineer of the canals,) for two hours, and instruct his son and daughter and two apprentices in drawing—I then snap up a hasty breakfast, (sometimes I go without,) and at ten o'clock go to the Rev. Mr. Cames's academy, where I attend, for one hour, four young gentlemen in drawing, one of whom is a young baronet, Sir Charles Levinge—from thence, at eleven o'clock, I go to Mrs. Clark's boarding school, and teach drawing to five young ladies—thence to Miss Grey's boarding school, at twelve o'clock, where I have eleven young ladies at draw-ing—and at one o'clock I go to Mr. Acres's, where I stay till four, and attend to the education of his two daughters, in English grammar, writing, arithmetic, geography, drawing, and French ; here I am a great favourite with my employer, who is the most opulent man in the town, and often dine and spend the evening with him ; he is an intimate friend of Mr.

Telford's, who recommended me to him—and I make no
doubt, would provide me some good situation in the country
if I had occasion to look out for one. After Christmas, I am
to get the writing master's business at Mrs. Clarke's school,
and to undertake the French class at Miss Grey's, both of
which can be attended in the evenings. . . . You
see I am pretty busy every day, and, indeed, my health
is not quite so good as in the summer, when I had more long
walks, and longer days to do my business in—but I do not
complain—when I consider the shattered state of my consti-
tution two or three years ago ; and it gives me infinite
satisfaction to find myself in possession of so ample an income,
after the starvation I was obliged for a time to undergo in
Dublin. As to society and amusement, there, indeed, I am very
deficient ; I have no acquaintances here to pass a vacant hour
with, except one, a young Scotchman, who is head gardener
to Lord Charleville, and who comes from near Annan—and
him I see very seldom. Books are therefore my only resource,
and even them I find difficult to procure, as the Irish are not
fond of reading, and would sooner expend a guinea in whiskey
punch than half-a-crown in a bookseller's shop. The only
evenings I spend 'out of my lodgings, are at Miss Grey's,
where her governesses and her young ladies are very sociable,
and either get me to a harmless game at cards, or provide me
with some amusing book to read for them. Sometimes I am
requested by Miss Grey to teach her young folks a dialogue
out of a play, and when any of their parents or friends drop
in, they are generally called upon to exhibit their perform-
ances, of which, and of my instructions, all parties seem very
proud. To tell you the truth, Miss Grey, a fine, jolly clever
woman, about forty, would, I am well convinced, have no
objection to make me the master of herself and her school—
but—I don't know—I don't seriously think of such a thing—
it would make me an Irishman for life—and besides—the lady
is a Roman catholic. I believe I shall jog on as I am till
circumstances permit me to come and lay my bones quietly in
Saint Mary's church-yard.

Now, my dear Bella, I have filled up a long letter with a vast deal of egotism as usual, and perhaps a little nonsense. . . . Meanwhile don't you forget to write soon.—Yours most affectionately, M. LONSDALE.

The next letter was addressed to his nephew and namesake, who had gone out as a Cadet in the East India Company's service.

TULLAMORE, (IRELAND), *2nd April*, 1811.

MY DEAR NEPHEW,—It gave me infinite concern that I was not able to send you a line in answer to that addrest to me on your departure for India. I was at that time confined to my bed by illness; and I believe the idea of not having given you a parting word or two, so hung upon my mind that it partly retarded my recovery. Since then, however, I have been in tolerable health till within these few days, and truth to say I am not at present able to write such a letter as I wish, but the opportunity that offers of sending it, impels me to do something, judging that whether it be little or much, you will be glad to hear from one who regards you with friendship and affection, and who is very anxious that *one* Emigrant from the Carlisle stock shall in due time return thither with improved fortune and fair character. My own endeavours, incessant and laborious as they have been, have given me nothing to boast of but a tolerable knowledge of mankind, and the other materials of which the world about us is made of ; and in exchange for a ruined fortune, all I have got is experience, at a time when it is too late to profit by it on my own account. Happy should I be and content with my own lot (for I am now accustomed to it) if I could impart some of that experience to the young relatives I find growing up about me, and turn my misfortunes to their advantage.

My dear namesake, I have much to say to you. I have since your departure often imagined myself talking with you on the subject of your conduct in the line of life you have entered into ; but this is not the time to commit my observa-

tions to paper, for both time and spirits are wanting. I intend
to postpone that task till I have heard from you an account
of your situation, connexions, and feelings—as I think my
remarks may then be directed more to the point you wish. In
the meanwhile I have heard so good an account of your talents
and disposition, that I have very little apprehension of your
deviating from the line of rectitude.   .   .   .   .   .

I really believe that for a young man of a naturally good
disposition, and with no bad propensities, the army holds out
fewer temptations to what are called "little actions" or mean-
nesses, than any other profession.   There is a degree of manly
honesty in the character of a soldier, who holds in contempt
the subterfuges by which many a thriving tradesman raises
himself to affluence, at the expense of his morals.   Carefully
avoid therefore anything like selfishness or duplicity ; and as
I firmly believe you set out with sound principles and un-
tainted honour, so hold on to the last—and in any case that
admits a *doubt* as to the moral propriety of what you are about
to do, *never do it.* This is, I think, a maxim which Lord
Chesterfield strongly urges to the consideration of his son, and
a better no man can act upon.

Adieu, my dear Nephew—let me hear from you, and direct
to me at Carlisle.   This moment my letter is called for.

Your's with sincerest affection,   .

MARK LONSDALE.

The privacy necessarily attached to the situation
of tutor was ill suited to the habits and disposition
of one who had been manager in one of the leading
theatres of London.   His friends seemed to be
aware of this, and with a view of drawing him from
his seclusion, and obtaining the benefit of his ser-
vices and congenial society once more, obtained for
him a situation in the Theatre Royal, Drury Lane.
He, however, did not live long to enjoy this post,

for his constitution, never robust, gave way, and he
expired on Thursday evening, February 16th, 1815,
in London. His remains were deposited in the
church-yard on the south side of St. Clement Danes,
Strand, attended by many friends.

His writings in a collected form have never been
published, and it is extremely doubtful now, half a
century after his death, that they will ever be
gathered together. He has written much and well,
and it is a pity that the labours of such a man
should be lost to the world. No doubt from the
multifarious labours during the time he was engaged
at Sadler's Wells and Drury Lane, and the harrassing
nature of his avocations, he would have little time
to grapple any particular subject with the full force
of his power. He wanted many of the essential
requisites of an author—leisure, contentment, ab-
sence of worldly care, and, above all, retirement.
Yet, notwithstanding these wants, he has transmitted
to us marks of ability of a high order. About the
age of twenty-two, he produced *The Upshot*, one of
the ablest and most original poems that has yet
appeared in the Cumberland dialect. Anderson
(who held the piece in manuscript for some time,)
has been accused, and not without reason, for
taking some of the best characters in one of his
ballads from it. *The Upshot* was originally intended
for Hutchinson's History of Cumberland, but
arrived too late for insertion in that work. Ac-
cordingly it remained in manuscript till 1811, when

it first appeared in Jollie's "Sketch of Cumberland Manners and Customs."

But it was more as a writer of pieces adapted to the stage that Mark Lonsdale chiefly shone, and of these, all that have been handed down to us are mere fragments. The greater part of the songs in this collection has been gleaned from plays produced for Sadler's Wells between 1788 and 1793. The volume from which they are collected appears to have been printed for the use of the theatre alone, and consequently has now become a rare book. Some of the songs are adapted to old airs; whilst others have either been touched up or altogether remodelled after the manner in which Robert Burns was so great an adept, and by which means even *he* has added to his reputation. Most of these songs form a marked contrast to the other known productions of Mark Lonsdale. They possess more grace, gaiety, and refinement; more sprightly sparkling airiness, than might have been expected from the general character of his writings.

The time he left Carlisle for London is not exactly known, but it must have been somewhere about the year 1784, when about twenty-six years of age. He was too young, therefore, to have fully developed the latent powers of his mind, which were subseqently frittered away in the theatres of London, writing for his daily bread.

That fine song, *The Old Commodore*, which must ever rank amongst the first sea-songs in the English

language, was, in all probability, produced for Sadler's Wells. In one of the plays called *Mars'
Holiday*, I find that the character of the "Gouty Commodore" was performed by one Mr. Boyce. It has only recently, however, been printed as the production of Mark Lonsdale, although his relatives and some of the older inhabitants of Caldewgate have long been aware of the real authorship. Indeed, so little care has been taken of the manuscripts, that I have been informed by one who was well acquainted with the family, sufficient material for at least two volumes has been either lost or destroyed. Diligent search has been made, but not a vestige can be found, and it is more than probable that the public have now received all they ever will receive of the writings of this remarkable man.

LOVE IN CUMBERLAND.

AIR : "Cuddle me, Cuddy."

EY, Jwohn, what'n manishment's 'tis
  'At tou's gaen to dee for a hizzy !
I hard o' this tarrible fiss,
An' I's cum't to advise the'—'at is ee.

Mun ! thou'll nobbet lwose t'e gud neame
  Wi' gowlin an' whingein' sae mickle ;
Cockswunters ! min, bide about heame,
  An' let her e'en gae to auld Nickle.

Thy plew-geer's aw liggin how-strow,
  An' somebody's stown thee thy couter ;
Oh faiks ! thou's duin little 'at dow
  To fash theesel ivver about her.

Your Simey hes brokken car stang,
  An' mendit it wid a clog-coaker ;
Pump-tree's geane aw whyte wrang,
  An' they've sent for auld Tommy Stawker.

Young filly's dung ower the lang stee,
An' leam'd peer Andrew the Theeker ;
Thee mudder wad suffer't for tee,
An' I hedn't happ'n't to cleek her.

Thou's spoilt for aw manner o' wark :
Thou nobbet sits peghan an' pleenan.
Odswucke, man ! doff that durty sark,
An' pretha gi'e way git a clean 'an !

An' then gow to Carel wi' me,—
Let her gang to Knock-cross wid her scwornin',—
Sec clanken at market we'll see,
I'll up'od ta' forgit her 'or mwornin' !

THE OLD COMMODORE.

[This famous sea-song has been issued in most song books published during the last fifty years, without any writer's name attached to it. I have, however, gathered sufficient evidence in Carlisle to warrant me in printing it as the production of Mark Lonsdale. There is still living in Caldewgate an old gentleman who has heard it sung dozens of times to Mark Lonsdale's brother John, and who says that it was always definitely spoken of as having been written by him. After gathering this and other testimonies of a like nature, I found that Thomas Dibdin had printed it as "written by Mark Lonsdale" in an edition of Sea-songs by his father and others. Testimony from such a quarter, respecting a contemporary sea-song, cannot be gainsayed. — *The Old Commodore* has been set to music by W. Reeve.]

Odsblood ! what a time for a seaman to skulk
  Under gingerbread hatches ashore !
What a damn'd bad job that this batter'd old hulk
  Can't be rigg'd out for sea once more.
    For the puppies as they pass,
    Cocking up a quizzing glass
  Thus run down the old Commodore :
    " That's the Old Commodore,
    The rum old Commodore,
  The gouty old Commodore—he, he !
    Why, the bullets and the gout
    Have so knock'd his hull about,
  That he'll never more be fit for sea."

Here I'm in distress, like a ship water logg'd,
  Not a tow-rope at hand, nor an oar ;
I am left by my crew, and may I be flogg'd,
  If that doctor shall physic me more !*
    While I'm swallowing his slops
    How nimble are his chops,
  Thus queering the old Commodore :
    " A bad case Commodore,
    Can't say, Commodore,
  Mustn't flatter, Commodore," says he,
    " For the bullets and the gout
    Have so knock'd your hull about,
  That you'll never more be fit for sea."

---

* VARIATION.—But that doctor's the son of a— !

What ! no more afloat ? blood and fury thev "
I'm a seaman and only threescore ;
And if, as they tell me, I'm likely to die,
Gadzooks ! let me not die ashore.
    As for death, 'tis all a joke,
    Sailors live in fire and smoke,
So at least says an old Commodore ;
    The rum old Commodore,
    The tough old Commodore,
The fighting old Commodore—he ! he !
    Whom the devil nor the gout,
    Nor the French dogs to boot,
Shall kill—till they grapple him at sea.

MARGERY TOPPING.

[From the "*Spanish Rivals*, a Musical Farce, as performed at the Theatre Royal, Drury Lane. Composed by Thomas Linley." 1784?—A copy of this work is in the library of the British Museum.]

When I was in Cumberland I went a-wooing,
But love to my sorrow had nigh been my ruin ;
I was dying by inches, and look'd so shocking,
And all for the sake of one Margery Topping.
    Alas ! dear Margery, Margery Topping.

When thinking of her so handsome and proper,
I sobb'd all the day and I set by my supper ;
My mother cried, " Peter, nay make thyself easy ;"
But that wasn't Margery,—(ah ! lack-a-daisy,)—
      Sweet Margery, Margery Topping.

I plucked up my heart, and I ask'd this maiden
If ever she thought it would come to a wedding ;
She look'd in my face, and she call'd me a " Ninny ;"
" Have thee !" quoth Margery, " No, not for a
    guinea !"
      O cruel Margery, Margery Topping !

Thought I to myself, what the devil can ail her,
I wonnet stay here, but I'll gang for a sailor ;
So I went my ways, and I writ in a letter,
" Oh ! fare-thee-well Meg, till thou likest me better,"
      O scornful Margery, Margery Topping !

———

LAST MARTINMAS GONE A YEAR.

[From the " Spanish Rivals."]

Last Martinmas gone a year,
    Odzooks ! how pleas'd was I,
When hiring day was come,
    And flails were all flung by ;

Our hearts and heels were light,
 We danc'd, an' we were mad,
Wi' every lad his lass,
 And every lass her lad.

Ay, you'd hae laugh'd to see,
'Twas neither heck nor gee,
As the fiddler shog'd his knee,
Tee iddle tee dump tee dee ;
 Wi' a whoop, lads, whoop,
 And hey for bonnie Cumberland !

I'se ne'er forget the time,
 I went to Rosley fair,
Wi' a pair of new sol'd pumps,
 To dance when I got there ;
How I o'th' auld grey nag,
 Was mounted like a king,
And Dick ran on before,
 Wi' Hawkie in a string.

Then soon as I'd selt my cow,
 And drunk till I was fou,
Wi' " Neighbour, how's a' wi' "—
 And " Neighbour, how's wi' you ?"
Tee iddle tee dump tee dee ;
 Wi' a whoop, lads, whoop,
 And hey for bonnie Cumberland !

WHEN THE BRAVE WOULD WIN THE FAIR.

[From the "Spanish Rivals."]

What impels to gallant deeds
Like a heart replete with love ?
He no threat'ning danger fears,
Who a noble mind will prove :
    All are trifles light as air,
    When the brave would win the fair.

'Twas for this I shunn'd repose,
Forc'd by adverse fate to prove,
Danger which the soldier knows,
Who fights for glory and for love :
    All are trifles light as air,
    When the brave would win the fair.

THE GALLANT WAITING MEN.

[From the "Spanish Rivals."]

The gallant waiting men in town,
    Address me as a goddess fair,
Yet what of that ? 'tis better known,
    I'm but as other women are :

Ne'er shilly shally can I wait,
　　When choice of lovers come to woo ;
But as I wish to change my state,
　　Why, let the best e'en buckle to ! ˙

My good old granny often said,
　　(And now I speak it frank and free,)
That men were for the women made,
　　And surely one was made for me :
But should I find my spousy naught,
　　As many better women do,
Ne'er think I want my lesson taught,
　　Depend upon't I'll fit him too.

———

STILL THE LARK FINDS REPOSE.

[From the "Spanish Rivals."]

Still the lark finds repose
　　In the full waving corn,
Or the bee on the rose,
　　Tho' surrounded with thorn :
Never robb'd of their ease,
　　They are thoughtless and free,
But no more gentle peace,
　　Shall e'er harbour with me.

Still the lark finds repose
In the full waving corn,
Or the bee on the rose,
Tho' surrounded with thorn :
While in search of delight,
Ev'ry pleasure they prove,
Ne'er tormented by pride,
Or the slights of fond love.

JACK'S THE LAD.

[From "The Songster's Multum Parvo. London : Knevett,
Arliss, and Baker."—About 1809. It is there put forth
anonymously, as Mark Lonsdale's songs generally were in
collections of that date.]

Our ship's a-port, so here I be,
With a heart as light as cork, d'ye see.
'Pon larboard quarter, Poll is jigging,
Dress'd in all her Sunday rigging ;
Wench and fiddle always make a sailor glad.
Old Nipperkin the landlord, keeps the grog afloat,
And kindly is the liquor handed down each throat ;
For if ever sailor took delight in
Swigging, kissing, dancing, fighting :
Damme ! I'll be bold to say that Jack's the lad.
With my tol de rol, de rol, &c.

Cheerly, my hearts ! ye know Jack Spry,
So full of romps and riggs, that I—
D'ye hear the merry fiddle going ?
Blood ! it sets me off a-toeing—
    That's he, Catgut—College Hornpipe, brisk old
       dad ;
Now for a reel—Sir David Hunter Blair—that's
       Scotch ;
Or Langolee ; or any thing but French or Dutch.
For if ever fellow took delight in
Swigging, kissing, dancing, fighting :
    Damme ! I'll be bold to say that Jack's the lad.
              With my tol de rol, &c.

My locker's rich !—the devil a mite ;
Why here's a pretty rig—Yes, I'm right ;
An old friend, like a blubbering ninny,
Look'd distress'd·like ; got my guinea.
    Can't help sniv'lling somehow, when I see folk sad ;
But howsomever should I've luck to fall once more,
'Long-side a Monseer, homeward bound, he'll pay
       the score.
For if ever fellow took delight in
Swigging, kissing, dancing, fighting :
    Damme ! I'll be bold to say that Jack's the lad.
              With my tol de rol, &c.

Huzza ! a gun—the signal's made,
All hands on board, the anchor's weigh'd ;
Lord ! how the girls by scores are flying
Fore and aft, all sobbing, crying,
    Thoughts of parting makes 'em all run roaring mad ;
But honor bids her gallant sons to glory go ;
So off again we scud, to lick the saucy foe.
For if ever fellow took delight in
Swigging, kissing, dancing, fighting :
    Damme ! I'll be bold to say that Jack's the lad.
             With my tol de rol, &c.

THE ENGLISH SAILOR.

[From the Play of "The Comic Extravaganza," as per-
formed at Sadler's Wells Theatre, 1793. It is there stated
that "the whole of the Dialogues, Songs, &c., are written and
arranged by Mark Lonsdale."]

Come, friend, sheer off with your fine slack jaw,
Or I'll make your crazy sides to yaw—
D'ye think for to hum good subjects so ?
        Why, man, 'tis all my eye !

You may shew your trinkums where you may,
I'm a plain Jack Tar—Bet—that's my way !
And to all that a foreign swab can say,
        Why, I sings fal de ral.

It was neither the girls, nor drink, nor debt,
Drove me to sea, now, was it, Bet?
I said it then, and I says so yet,
   'Twas all to sarve my king.

Then damme ! why should a French *monseer*
E'er come with a yarn to say this here—
That an English heart has *that** to fear,
   While he sings fal de ral.

Now, because I'm a-gigging it here ashore,
You may think I goes to sea no more ;
And I don't, d'ye mind, blame you therefore,
   'Cause I should a-said the same.

But, lord ! I'm none of your skulking swells,
Tho' I likes a trip to Sadler's Wells—
And there, when I sees the beaux and belles,
   Why, I sings fal de ral.

Then, Bet, my girl, since my mind you know,
Let's take one spell before we go,
All hands on deck for a dance—yo ! ho !
   Why, fiddlers, that's your sort.

Should a true Jack Tar up aloft there be,
Mayhap he'd like to join with me,
Take a parting frisk—then off to sea,
   And there sing fal de ral.

   * Snaps his fingers.

THE THREE POOR FISHERMEN.

[From the Play of "The Savages." Sadler's Wells, 1792.
—Respecting this song Mr. Chappell has furnished me with
the following note : "The first verse and the burden are
a paraphrase of *We be Three Poor Mariners*, one of those
Freemen's Songs which were so much in vogue in the reign
of Henry the VIII., and which that monarch delighted to
sing with his courtiers."]

We be three poor fishermen,
　Who daily troll the seas ;
We spend our lives in jeopardy,
　While others live at ease.
The sky looks black around, around,
　The sky looks black around,
And he that would be merry, boys,
　Come haul his boat aground.

We cast our lines along the shore
　In stormy wind and rain ;
And every night we land our nets,
　Till daylight comes again.
The sky looks black around, around,
　The sky looks black around,
And he that would be merry, boys,
　Come haul his boat aground.

HEY HO! DOWN DERRY.

[From the Play of " The Hall of Augusta ; or, The Land we live in." Sadler's Wells, 1793.—This song appears to have been moddled from Shakspeare's *Sigh no more ladies, sigh no more*, especially the chorus.]

Mistaken Britons, rail no more,
  Born to every blessing,
Fear'd at sea, and lov'd on shore,
  The best of kings possessing :
Then gloom not so, but nobly shew
  That you're both wise and merry,
Converting all your fancy'd woe
  To hey, ho ! down derry.

Mistaken Britons, rail no more,
  For foreign fancies grieving,
Do that your fathers did before,
  Support the land you live in :
Then gloom not so, but nobly shew
  That you're both wise and merry,
Converting all your fancy'd woe,
  To hey, ho ! down derry.

THE DEIL GAE WI' THEM.

(OLD WITCHES' SONG.)

[From the Play of "The Witch of the Lakes." Sadler's Wells, 1793.]

When troubles surround thee and dangers are rife,
Tak' this wooden spurtle and fight for thy life ;
It'll save thee and serve thee, and mak' thy foes flee,
And a plague gang wi' them that meddles wi' thee.

A whirl of thy gulley has sae mickle pow'r—
It'll baffle misfortune, tho' never so sour ;
It'll work many wonders right unco to see,
And a plague gang wi' them that tooly wi' thee.

O'er mountain and moor, o'er causeway and bog,
Let the auld farren laird hae the life o' a dog ;
Whip aff wi' his daughter right pawkey and flee,
And the deil gae wi' them that fashes wi' thee.

COME HERE YE WITCHES.

[From the Entertainment of "Medea's Kettle." Sadler's Wells, 1792.]

Come here ye witches wild and wanton,
The woods and dreary pathways haunting,
Ye, who mark'd with evil omen,
Gambol forth in shapes uncommon.

Badger, weasel, hog, or hare,
Or tiger-cat, or wolf or bear,
In hut or hole, or cave or den,
Or ditch or brake, or field or fen ;
Screeching, roaring, grinning, growling,
Grunting, whistling, hooting, howling ;
If in shape of beast ye be,
Shake it off and follow me.

Let our revenge yon fools pursue,
That dar'd to sport with me and you ;
Let deadly spells unite to snare 'em,
Then torment and never spare 'em.
Hags that go like hog or hare,
Or tiger-cat, or wolf or bear,
In hut or hole, or cave or den,
Or ditch or brake, or field or fen ;
Screeching, roaring, grinning, growling,
Grunting, whistling, hooting, howling ;
If in shape of beast ye be,
Shake it off and follow me.

THE SPINNING WHEEL.

[From "The Prize of Industry." Sadler's Wells, 1793.—
" I see that this song," writes Mr. Chappell, " is to the tune
and in the measure of the following :

'To ease his heart, and own his flame,
Blythe Jockey to young Jenny came ;
But tho' she liked him passing weel,
She careless turn'd her spinning wheel.'

These words were written to a favorite Scotch air (so called,
but not really Scotch,) in the Overture to *Thomas and Sally*,
and composed by Dr. Arne. The air was long popular, and
that no doubt was the inducement for Mark Lonsdale to write
new words to it."]

How blest the maid whose blythesome heart,
Ne'er felt the pangs of Cupid's dart,
Whose eyes from slumber lightly steal—
And cheerful turns her spinning wheel :

But, ah ! when once the urchin foe
Has aim'd aright his luckless bow,
What pains are we condemn'd to feel—
How slowly turns the spinning wheel.

Oh ! time, how swift thy moments flew
When Jamie first my notice drew !
As at my feet he used to kneel,
How gaily went my spinning wheel !

But mad ambition drew him far,
To brave the horrid chance of war ;
He left me here in woeful weal,
And dully goes my spinning wheel.

LOVELY FANNY.

[From "The Prize of Industry," a Musical Entertainment. Sadler's Wells, 1793.]

When first my country claim'd my aid,
 And from my cottage tore me far,
I for a musket chang'd my spade,
 And sought the terrors of the war ;
Whilst martial glory fir'd my breast,
One thought still robb'd my soul of rest,
 The thought of lovely Fanny.

When round my head the winds blew high,
 And hostile bullets whistled drear ;
When cannons thunder'd thro' the sky,
 For her alone my heart knew fear :
When fortune crown'd my ceaseless toils,
One thought alone endear'd her smiles,
 The thought of lovely Fanny.

Ah ! should she then her faith maintain,
 And spurn at av'rice—sordid lure !
With her I'll seek the rural plain,
 Nor once regret though we are poor :
Then, as ambition I resign,
Indulge this fav'rite thought of mine,
 The thought of lovely Fanny.

WHEN THE SUN RISES CHEERFULLY.

[From the " Prize of Industry."]

When the sun rises cheerfully over the lawn,
My face still is dimpl'd and smiles like the dawn,
And I bound to my labour as brisk as a fawn ;
　　No sighing or pining,
　　No moping or whining,
I laugh, dance, and sing with a heart full of glee.

Should the lads who in whimpers my beauty declare,
In secret tell others they're doubly as fair,
I never go drooping about with despair ;
　　Nor sighing nor pining,
　　Nor moping nor whining,
But laugh, dance, and sing with my heart full of glee.

———

GIGGLE-DOWN FAIR.

[From the play of "The Savages." Sadler's Wells, 1792.]

Come neighbours, awhile leave your labours and care,
And follow tight Andrew to Giggle-down Fair,
Such din and diversion you never did see
As to-day—if you choose to give credit to me ;
　　Come away, come away, come away to the fair,
　　　In your holiday gear,
　　　Trim and dainty appear,
Come away, come away to the fair.

You may there see a minuet danc'd on the wire,
And a conjuror swallow a basin of fire ;
Thro' a glass, for a halfpenny, see a fine show,
Or behold for a groat tame wild-beasts all a-row.
             Come away, come away, &c.

Here, a pack of strange fools thro' a collar do grin,
He that makes the worst faces is surest to win ;
With hot hasty pudding see some cramm'd to their
     eyes,   .
And he that's best scalded walks off with the prize.
             Come away, come away, &c.

Then I and my master can cure all your ills,
With our ointments, potions, our powders and pills ;
For, as well as great doctors who take their degrees,
Tho' we do no good, we can pocket the fees.
             Come away, come away, &c.

JOHN STAGG,

THE BLIND BARD OF WIGTON.

1770—1823.

JOHNNY BROWN AND GRANNY BELL.

OLD Johnny Brown liv'd up yon hill,
    Old Granny Bell liv'd on the moor ;
    Now, Johnny Brown was very rich,
But Granny Bell was very poor :

His coffers groan'd with hoarded wealth,
    His spacious barns were fill'd with corn,
Unnumber'd flocks were in his fold ;
    But greedier wretch was never born.

Poor Granny Bell was turn'd fourscore,
    Bent down with age and poverty ;
Decrepid grown, and weak with want,
    The poorest of the poor was she.

Hence from their various fates ensued,
 Of being poor, and being rich,
That Johnny Brown was reckon'd wise,
 And Granny Bell was call'd a witch.

In bleak December, when the snows
 Deep drifted o'er the moors, were spread,
She hobbl'd up to Johnny's house,
 To beg a morsel of his bread :

" Do, do, good neighbours ! do," she cried,
 " My wants with pitying eyes, behold ;
A morsel spare me ; or I die—
 O'ercome with hunger and with cold.

" For once, some kindly comfort give,
 The wint'ry blasts ; hark ! how they roar !
Short is my journey to the grave—
 Perhaps, I'll trouble you no more ! "

" Aroint thee, witch !" quoth Johnny Brown,
 " Now, by the mass ! that must not be ;
For had I ten times what I have,
 I would not give a mite to thee."

Stung with this sharpness of reply,
 In mutt'ring tone the caitiff swore ;
And pray'd his substance, kyth and kin,
 That heav'n would never prosper more,

He heard her execrations dire,
　　They fill'd his inmost soul with dread :
Next morning brought the doleful news,
　　The best milk-cow he had was dead ;

Ere noon his son to market sent,
　　He heard by rogues had been beguil'd ;
His wife, ere ev'ning told him, too,
　　Their eldest daughter was with child.

" Now, by my sooth !" says Johnny Brown,
　　The beldam bears me mickle spite ;
But, ere such mischief I'll endure,
　　I'll shoot the witch this very night ! "

The night was hush'd, the moon shone clear,
　　The air was keen as keen could be,
When Johnny Brown his firelock took,
　　And out with deadly wrath went he.

In ev'ry corner that he pass'd,
　　Around the hay-rick and the well,
He look'd with curious eye, in hopes
　　To find poor hapless Granny Bell.

At length, between him and the light,
　　He thought he saw the wish'd-for game ;
" Yes, yes ! she's there !" quoth Johnny Brown,
　　So straightway took his vengeful aim !

Off went the piece, unerring, true,
  The bullet whistl'd thro' the air ;
With speed he ran to seize the prize,
  But, lo ! he'd shot his best grey mare !

Thus foil'd for once, went Johnny Brown,
  Home to his house, with burning gall ;
But swore, if morning light were come,
  To burn the witch, her house, and all.

The foul design so fill'd his mind,
  That e'en tho' fast asleep, he rose,
And snatch'd a firebrand from the hearth,
  And to his fatal purpose goes.

His wife she miss'd him from her side,
  She rose with haste, the cause to learn ;
There spied she luckless Johnny Brown
  Just setting fire to his own barn.

She shriek'd right loud, as well she might,
  The husband 'woke with this alarm ;
But, in the moment of surprize,
  Poor Johnny fell, and broke his arm !

What mischiefs happen'd Johnny Brown,
  In consequence of Granny Bell ;
From first to last, to him and his,
  I'm sure, are more than I can tell.

II.   3

"Now foul befal the hellish hag,
  (Quoth Johnny Brown) she doth me twitch,
But, if there's justice in the land,
  I will exterminate the witch."

So said, next morning with the light
  Vindictive Johnny Brown arose ;
And with his neighbours and his friends,
  To seek the hapless beldam goes.

But disappointed was their rage,
  No witch to torture they behold ;
For on a lowly straw-made couch,
  Lay Granny Bell, both stiff and cold !

A BALLAD OF BROUGHAM CASTLE.

[Brougham Castle, which stands on the borders of West-
morland, near the banks of the river Eamont, and about two
miles from Penrith, is one of the most imposing ruins in the
north of England. The Black Fell, where dwelt "the weird
woman," forms part of a chain of mountains running on the
east of Cumberland.]

Fair shone the moon o'er Brougham's tower,
  And fair on Eamont's streams,
And fair down Eden's fertile vale,
  Far shone its lengthening beams ;

When Lady Eleanor arose,
   And listless left her bed ;
For peace her pillow had forsook,
   And slumber from her fled.

And she has climbed the highest tower,
   And traced the turrets round ;
And she has sighed, and she has wept,   `
   But ease has no where found.

" Ah, me ! (she said) was e'er before
   So sad forlorn a wife ?
For though I am Lord Herbert's spouse,
   I lead a widowed life.

" Twelve tedious months are past and gone,
   Since last he left these arms :
O'er distant shores he wins afar,
   'Midst danger and alarms.

" Ye gentle gales that round me blow,
   Augmented by my sighs,
Oh ! gently waft him home again,
   To cheer these longing eyes !

" For here, with anxious sad distress
   My nights are passed away ;
And cheerless solitude and grief
   Attend me through the day.

"But if the morning dawn were come,
    Full quickly would I ride
To the weird woman, where she dwells,
    Close by the Black Fell side.

"There with her will I counsel take,
    Her forecast's famed on far,
To know when he, Lord Herbert, shall
    Forsake the cruel war."

Lord Herbert he on Syria's shores
    With martial squadrons sped
With princely Edward, to the fight
    The Christian forces led.

Much by his prince approved was he,
    Much by his peers renown'd ;
For through the host of Christian knights
    A braver was not found.

Destruction followed where he led
    And marked his furious course ;
Nor could the Saracen's whole power
    Check his resistless force.

Up with the light rose Eleanor ;
    She's ta'en the swiftest steed,
And quickly she to Black Fell side
    Has posted with all speed.

And soon she's gained the fated place,
  And soon an entrance found ;
And the weird woman soon has met,
  For forecast far renown'd.

" O Lady, say, (the beldam cried,)
  What brings you here so soon ?"
"I come (dame Eleanor replied)
  From you to beg a boon ;

"Which you must grant ere I depart,
  Or else must go with me ;
And as your 'bodings shall betide,
  So shall your guerdon be."

"What would'st thou have, sweet Lady fair ?
  What would'st thou understand?
For, be assured, what I can do
  Thou freely may'st command."

" My husband, brave Lord Herbert, he
  Now wins on Syria's plains ;
Fain would I know his plight and how
  This warfare he sustains."

" Then back to Brougham you must hie,
  (Replied the wither'd crone ;)
And all that you would learn, shall there
  To you be fully known.

"Spur on your palfrey with all speed,
  Nor stop, nor make delay ;
I shall be there as soon as you,
  So, Lady, post away."

Now, Lady Eleanor thus warned,
  Has homeward turned her steed ;
O'er hill and dale, o'er bog and burn,
  To Brougham with all speed.

And when she passed the castle-moat,
  Who readier was to wait
Than the weird-woman of Black Fell side,
  All at the castle gate !

And she has lighted from her steed,
  And entered by the hall ;
And she has to the chamber passed,
  The sybil, too, withal.

And she has bolted fast the door,
  All with a silver pin,
That none without might hear or see,
  And no one might come in.

"And now, I'll tell thee, Lady fair,
  (The caitiff said with speed,)
What things must first be done, ere we
  Can with our spell proceed.

"And first with vinegar and meal
  Yourself must knead a cake,
Which on the embers must be laid,
  That it may slowly bake.

"Then hie to some south-running stream,
  Of no man ask you leave,
But take your shift, and in the brook
  There wash well the left sleeve.

"Then haste you back, and hang the same
  Before the fire to dry ;
What of the process yet remains
  We'll finish by and by.

" Wait 'till the castle-bell strikes One,
  Nor dash'd nor daunted be ;
For be assured that at that hour
  Lord Herbert you shall see."

Slow wind their way the tedious hours ;
  Slow passed the parting day ;
And anxious grew dame Eleanor
  At midnight's tardy stay.

.   .   .   .   .

At length the castle-bell tolled One ;
  The stately mansion shook ;
The doors were burst !—Lord Herbert stood
  With stern revengeful look ;

In arms accoutred cap-a-pie,
   With sword and buckler bright ;
And gaily harness'd, as became
   A gallant Christian knight.

And he has ta'en and turn'd the cake
   That on the embers burn'd ;
And eke the shift before the hearth
   As carefully has turned.

Then up and crew the shrill-voic'd cock,
   The sable and the grey ;—
Lord Herbert rushed forth from the hall ;
   Nor longer might he stay :

But as with hasty stride he flew
   Forth at the chamber door,
Lord Herbert in his hurry dropp'd
   His sword upon the floor ;

And sythe was heard a hollow groan,
   And eke a mournful sigh ;
The Lady she took up the sword,
   And careful put it by.

But sadly sank the Lady's heart,
   Now that the shade was gone ;
And sadly seemed she to repent
   The deed that she had done.

Two ling'ring, anxious, irksome years
  A widow'd bride she mourn'd :
At length Lord Herbert with the Prince
  And England's pow'rs return'd.

Straight to the Hall the Baron flew,
  Nor made he stop or stay ;
And Lady Eleanor, I ween,
  Was joyful on that day.

The costliest banquet was prepar'd ;
  The minstrels shook the hall ;
The copious bowl was push'd around,
  And mirth pervaded all.

For all to see the Lord's return,
  Express'd unfeign'd delight ;
Whilst he resolv'd that ev'ry heart
  Should feel no care that night.

It chanc'd that on a future day,
  Lord Herbert, ranging round
The various chambers of the dome,
  His sword, ill-fated ! found :

With horror he the weapon view'd,
  With rage, and wild surprize ;
For well he knew the luckless blade,
  Yet, scarce could trust his eyes.

But swift he from the chamber hies,
  The falchion in his hand;
And of fair Lady Eleanor
  Thus sternly does demand;

" Where got'st thou that fair sword, Lady?
  Now tell me, on thy word :
From what young knight, or warrior wight,
  Dame, got'st thou that fair sword?"

" Why sternly dost thou thus enquire,
  Lord Herbert, this from me?
Within your armoury, good sooth !
  Great store of swords there be !

" Swords are not things for women's use !
  Then, why this question? say ;—
You look most angrily, my lord !
  What is the reason, pray?"

" Where got'st thou that fair sword, Lady?
  Now, tell me, on thy word ;
From what young knight, or warrior wight,
  Dame, got'st thou that fair sword?"

" My Lord, if I must say the truth,
  And tell you on my word,
I almost durst be bound to swear
  It is my Father's sword."

"No, no! 'tis not Lord Osrick's sword;
   I know that blade too well:
Thou shalt not thus prevaricate,
   But truth be forc'd to tell."

"Doth it become Lord Herbert's wife
   To tamper him with lies?
Or doth it suit Lord Herbert's wife
   His menace to despise?"

"Where got'st thou that fair sword, Lady?
   Now tell me on thy word;
From what young knight, or warrior wight,
   Dame, got'st thou that fair sword?"

Then down upon her bended knees
   Dame Eleanor did fall;
And, barring parley or disguise,
   The Lady told him all.

.   .   .   .

"Wretch that thou art! (Lord Herbert said,)
   I knew the sword was mine!
Death is too slight a punishment
   For such a fault as thine:

"Not all the torments hell contains,
   That most the damn'd dismay,
Can parallel the pangs I felt
   On that unhappy day!

" Whirl'd like a thunderbolt along,
    O'er ocean, earth, and air,
O'er craggy steeps, and bri'ry brakes,
    To rest I knew not where.

" Whilst all the time my body lay
    On earth, devoid of breath !
And all around the battle press'd,
    And threaten'd certain death.

" 'Twas there on first recov'ring life,
    I vow'd, on knightly word,
That they should surely lose their lives
    With whom I found the sword !

.   .

" Then, die !"—so said, the fatal blade
    Deep pierc'd the shrieking wife !
She fell ; and at her husband's feet
    Surrender'd up her life !

———

THE HONEST SAILOR'S SONG.

Come listen to my jovial song
    Ye sons of stormy ocean,
Condemn me or commend me,
    As fancy leads your notion :

Though songsters frequently may err,
  Yet think me not a railer,
For though I am a shaggy dog
  Yet I'm an honest sailor.

When rattling thunders shake the air
  To fill the mind with horror,
And mariners dismay'd behold
  The scene with dread and terror :
When dreadful waves mountaineous roll,
  And tempests loud are howling,
A sailor, though a shaggy dog,
  Should ne'er be heard a-growling.

But patience, sirs, a while excuse
  The sad account I give you,
No dastard base am I, d'ye see,
  Therefore will not deceive you :
For sailing's now in fashion grown
  With every rank and station,
Since piracy and bartering are
  The business of the nation.

There scuds a lady of eighteen,
  With all her sails full spread, sirs,
Well rigg'd, d'ye see, from stem to stern,
  And bearing right a-head, sirs.;
But should some sprightly fopling buck
  Attack her starboard quarter,
She'd soon abandon piracy
  And heart for heart would barter.

The miser down his hatches shuts
   To all solicitations,
He values not the orphan's tears,
   Or widow's lamentations ;
But stupid as the boisterous main,
   He steers right off, and leaves 'em ;
Then to the devil steers his course,
   Who down hell's gang-way heaves him. ·

The holy parson from aloft
   Bawls out to Heaven for quarters,
To save a single sinking crew,
   Implores both saints and martyrs ;
But stop his pay, and then you'll see
   The ever zealous parson,
Will, (Bing like,) set his helm alee,
   And sinners turn his —— on.

The statesman, too, down folly's stream,
   Glides on with sails unbended,
But founders oft on credit's coast,
   Ere half his voyage is ended.
Split on the rocks of mortgages
   He's forc'd to steer abaft, sirs,
Whilst lawyers take the weather gauge
   And rake him fore and aft, sirs.

Thus all the world, as well as me,
   Are sailors in their kind, sirs,
Some, fool-like, stem the sea of life,
   Some drive before the wind, sirs :

One common harbour, though they seek,
　Yet are their courses various ;
Two founder, whilst one gains the port,
　The channel's so precarious.

————

THE RETURN.

A NORTH COUNTRY BALLAD.

Fast the patt'ring hail was fa'ing,
　And the sowping rain as thick ;
Loud and snell the whurlwind bla'ing,
　While the neeght was dark as pick :

When upon her strea couch liggan
　Susan steep'd her waukryfe ee'n,
And about her crazy biggin'
　Rwoar'd the hollow whurlblast keen.

In each arm a bairn lay sleepin' ;
　I' their luiks lank famine sat,
And their een seem'd blear'd wi' weepin',
　For the things they seldom gat.

On her lwonely bed she toss'd her
　Darkin' till the tempest ceas'd ;
But, peer lass ! nea change of posture
　Calm'd the conflict of her breast.

In her feace, a heart sair anguish'd
    Meeght a stranger's eye survey;
Six dree years had Susan languish'd
    Sen her Walter went away.

He far owre the stormy ocean,
    Wan on India's distant shore;
Courtin' fortune and promotion,
    E'en amid the battle's rwoar.

Sair agean his inclination,
    Watty left his heame and ease,
Wife, bairns, and ilk kind relation
    To traverse the dang'rous seas;

Widow-like his absence mournin',
    Mony a sleepless neeght she past,
Prayin' aye his seafe returnin'
    As she lyth'd the lengthnin' blast.

    .   .   .   .   .

Yence the rwose and lily blended
    In fair Susan's bridal feace;
But fwok said, whea erst hed kent it,
    Sadly alter'd was the kease.

She whea leate sea doose and jolly
    Need hae turn'd her feace o' nane;
Suin thro' grief and melancholy
    Turns to parfect skin and beane:

" Cruel fate, thy mandate alter ! "
Oft she murmur'd in despair ;
" Give me ! give me, back my Walter !
Give me him ! I ask nea mair !

" Here disconsolate and weary
Are my days of sorrow past ;
And my neeghts forlorn and eery
That ilk yen I wish my last.

" But a spring of whope yet cheers me,
And our wee yen's yammerin' noise,
Mair than owte to life endears me,
Broodin' still some future joys.

" Hark ! the whurlblast loudy blusters,
Dreary howlin' owre my head,
And with rage the tempest musters
On my crazy clay-built shed.

" Wintry blasts, that bluster owre me,
Waft my sighs to Walter's ears ;
Gales auspicious, quick restwore me
Him whea's smiles can dry my tears.

" Fancy ! whither wadst thou lead me ?
Say, what phantoms to impart ?
Visionary shades owre-spread me
To amuse my love-lorn heart.

" There's my Walter's feace I view now,
   'Mid the leeght'nin's transcient glare ;
Pleasin' form, I'll thee pursue now,
   But 'tis geane, and I despair.

" Hark ! what shriek was that 'at mingl'd
   Wi' the liftan tempest-howl ?
On my ears like fate it jingl'd,
   Piercin' to my varra soul.

" Was it not my true love ca'ing ?
   Was't not like his weel-kent tone ?
Say, peer heart, where art thou fa'ing ?
   Fancy, say, where art thou gone ? "

Heavier now the tempest musters,
   Down in plennets teems the rain,
Louder, aye, the whurlblast blusters,
   Sweepin' owre the spacious plain.

Susan, fill'd wi' apprehension
   At the dismal, dang'rous rwoar,
Suin is fix'd in mute attention
   Wi' loud knockin's at her door.

" Susan, rise ! " a voice loud bawlin'
   Said, " Unbar the envious door ! "
" Whea commands ? " she scream'd, then fallin'
   Senseless, streek'd her on the floor.

Wi' a rounge the yieldin' hinges
    Frae the partin' stoothens flee,
In the storm-struck stranger swinges,
    Walter enters—yes, 'twas he !

Swift to Susan's aid he hies him,
    Greapin' roun' the weel kent bower,
Leeght the leeghtnin's flash supplies him,
    Her he spies upon the floor ;

In his arms he gently rears her,
    Softly lifts her droopin' head,
Anxious owre the room he bears her,
    And reclin'd her on the bed.

But his tongue was pinch'd to falter,
    " Wake ! my fair one, wake ! and see—
Wake ! and cheer thy long lost Walter,
    Seafe return'd to luive and thee ! "

Lang she sleeps not, strugglin' nature,
    Suin suspended life restwores ;
On his habit, form, and stature
    Wi' impatient wildness pores.

Frae his arms in deep confusion,
    Till her ingle swift she flies ;
Thinkin' this was a' illusion,
    That bewitch'd her ears and eyes.

Prodlin' up the smotherin' embers,
  Swift the sweelin' heather flies,
She nea trace of him remembers,
  Alter'd sair by his disguise.

Sowp'd wi' rain, wi' glore bespatter'd,
  Frowzy beard and visage wan,
Teated locks and garments tatter'd,
  Mair he seem'd of ghaist than man.

" Ah," cried he, "can time sae alter
  Fwoks, as thus to be forgot ?
Fair yen, I'm thy faithful Walter ;
  Canst thou, Susan, know me not ?"

When his weel-kent voice she listens,
  A' her doubts are suin supprest,
In her een keen transpwort glistens,
  And she sunk upon his breast.

Here awhile with ardour glowin'
  Stood the lover and his wife,
Beath their hearts wi' joy owre-flowing,
  Suin he kiss'd her into life.

" Yes," she said, " thou lang-lost stranger,
  Thou art still my husband dear ;
Seafe, I whope, return'd frae danger,
  And nea mair to leave me here.

" What tho' thou'rt wi' muck bespatter'd,
What tho' thou'rt in weafu' plight,
Matted locks and vestments tatter'd,
Still thou art my soul's delight."

.   .   .   .   .

"Know," said he, "tho' foul and tatter'd
In my present garb and graith ;
Tho' with muck and mire bespatter'd,
I've enough to bless us baith.

" Twice ten thousand pounds await me,
We s'all yet see happier days;
Yet nea rank s'all e'er elate me
Providence commands my praise.

" Midst the battle's devastation
Fell my captain, stunn'd with blows ;
I succeeded to his station,
By this chance my fortune rose.

" Wealth in heaps now seem'd to press me,
Honours wait me day and night,
Fortune seem'd resolv'd to bless me,
In amends for former spite.

" Thus with riches in abundance,
Suin I quitted India's shore,
And securin' that redundance,
Sought again my native shore.

" But of a' the joys I've teasted,
    Or mun e'er expect to teaste
In time to come, or time far weasted,
    This, this moment joys me meast.

"Suin as London port we enter'd
    Off I set without delay ;
Thro' the storms and tempests ventur'd
    Luive nea patience had for stay.

" Cheer thee, then, my Susan, cheer thee,
    Pleasure yet thy cheek shall cheer ;
Think thy Wat will aye be near thee ;
    Think thy luive will aye be near."

ROBERT ANDERSON.

AN AUTOBIOGRAPHY.*

T six o'clock on the snowy morning of
February 1st, 1770, I first beheld the
light of this world at the Dam Side, in
the suburbs of the ancient city of Carlisle ; a poor
little tender being, scarce worth the trouble of rear-
ing. Old Isbel, the midwife, entertained many fears
that I was only sent to peep around me, shed tears,
and then leave them. I was the youngest of nine
children, born of parents getting up in years, who
with all their kindred had been long kept in bond-
age by poverty.

At an early age I was placed in a charity school,
supported by the Dean and Chapter of Carlisle, for
children only. Well do I remember the neat dress,
slow speech, placid countenance, nay, every feature
of good old Mrs. Addison the teacher. In this
school I studied my letters, the see-saw drone of the

* Abridged from the edition of 1820.

primer, and waded through the reading-made-easy; and was then turned over to a long, lean pretender to knowledge. His figure was similar to that of the mad knight of La Mancha. Never have I perused Cervantes' inexhaustible treasury of humour without having my tutor in view. Impelled probably by necessity he devoted so much time to angling, that the few poor starved-looking scholars were shame-fully neglected. He always selected me to accom-pany him up the banks of the Eden or the Caldew; and I am led to suppose it was during our summer excursions that an attachment to rural scenery first stole over my youthful mind. My parents finding I did not make progress equal to their expectations, placed me under Mr. Isaac Ritson, in the Quaker's school; but in a few weeks that learned and in-genious young man left the city. I was then placed under my last and best tutor, Mr. Walter Scott, a learned and truly respectable character. Under this worthy man I made considerable progress in arithmetic; though to this necessary branch of edu-cation I always felt a strong aversion, and would much rather have pursued the study of grammar, of which I never attained any exact knowledge.

Among our neighbours was a decent industrious old woman, born in the Highlands of Scotland; and at her fireside I spent many a winter evening, delighted beyond measure with the wild Scottish ballads which she taught me, while labouring at her wheel. *Gilderoy, Johnny Armstrong, Sir James the Ross*, *Barbary Allan*, and *Binorie*, were great favorites. From this cheerful, kind-hearted creature, I imbibed the love of song, which has to the present day so particularly engaged my attention.

About the expiration of my tenth year it was judged necessary for me to quit the school, and try to earn something by hard labour, wherewith to assist a poor father, now infirm. I felt exceedingly rejoiced at this proposal; for being of a timid disposition I always crept to school trembling like a culprit going to receive punishment. My first labour was under one of my brothers, a calico printer; and at the end of the week well do I remember the happiness it afforded me to present my wages (one shilling and sixpence) to my father. My next change was to be bound apprentice to a pattern drawer in 1783, under the firm of T. Losh & Co., Denton Holme, near Carlisle; where I enjoyed all the happiness an industrious youth could hope for, being treated with every mark of esteem.

From childhood a love of rural life grew with me, and I let slip few opportunities of spending the Sabbath in some village during the summer. It was on paying a visit at a friend's house that I was first smitten with female charms; which then seemed greater to me than I can describe. Picture to yourself a diffident youth in his sixteenth year, daily pouring out the sighs of a sincere heart, for an artless rosy cottage girl, something younger than myself.

> She was all my thoughts by day,
> And all my dreams by night.

At church she drew my attention from the preacher ; and great was my mortification if she happened to be absent on my visit to the neighbourhood. Had my income—which was then barely sufficient to afford the necessaries of life—been adequate to my wishes, with what happiness could I have laid my fortune at her feet and offered myself for better and for worse : but fate decreed otherwise.

In the year 1794, being at Vauxhall Gardens, for the first time, I felt disgusted with many of the songs written in the mock pastoral Scottish style, and supposing myself capable of producing what might be considered equal or perhaps superior, on the following day I wrote four songs. *Lucy Gray* was my first attempt, and was suggested from hearing a Northumbrian rustic relate the story of two unfortunate lovers. To use the simple language of the relator : " Mony a smart canny lad wad hae gane far efter dark—aye thro' fire an' watter !—just to git a luik at her." These songs were set to music by Mr. Hook ; and my first poetic effusion was sung by Master Phelps, with great applause, and loudly encored.

My poor father, whom I had regularly supported, now paid me an unexpected visit. He was in his seventy-sixth year ; and walked from Carlisle to London, a distance of three hundred and one miles, in six days.* Tears of joy greeted our meeting; but such was his aversion to the noise and bustle of London that I could only prevail on him to remain a fortnight. I feel it impossible to write concerning him without shedding a tear; for the greatest happiness I enjoy, now in life's decline, is the reflection of having fulfilled my duty to him. Would to God, all who have it in their power would act in a similar manner to a helpless parent!

In 1798, ambition led me, like too many of my brother scribblers, to publish a volume of poems, which I dedicated to J. C. Curwen, Esq., M.P. From this publication I received little more than dear bought praise.

Already have I adverted to the pleasures rural life afforded; and my attention to the manners of the Cumbrian peasantry was now greater than ever. My only poetical delight has been the study of nature; and pleased am I when my Muse appears in her rustic dress. She has occasionally visited my lowly shed, arrayed in the mock trappings of grandeur; but that only called forth a smile, instead of thanks, from the humble Bard. . In December, 1801, I published the ballad called *Betty Brown* in the Cumberland dialect. The praise bestowed by many, but particularly by my friend Mr. Thomas Sanderson, encouraged me to other attempts in the

---

* This must be a mistake. Fifty miles a day for six consecutive days is no joke. A man of the same build and "lishness" as Christopher North might in his prime accomplish such a task; but surely not one seventy-six years old!

same species of poetry. At length a sufficient number of pieces were produced to form a volume, which was sent to the press under the title of "Cumberland Ballads." Mr. Sanderson kindly furnished notes to it. This publication did not at all improve my finances, as much of the subscription money was lost. The work, however, becoming somewhat popular, the edition was soon exhausted; and a new impression was sent into the world from the press of Mr. Hetherton of Wigton, who purchased the copyright. In 1808, another, and I am sorry to say, an incorrect edition, was published.

Prior to the second edition I left Carlisle to enter a situation at Brookfield, near Belfast. On reaching Dumfries, great was my anxiety to pay the tributary tear at the tomb of nature's bard, Robert Burns. It was this alone which induced me to prefer a journey through Scotland, to a short sail from Maryport. The morning was so tempestuous that it was with difficulty a friend conducted me to the corner where his remains were deposited. The deep snow hid the narrow mound, and the flat stone laid over it; but the trodden pathway shewed the respect paid by strangers to the bard's memory. The humble inscription did not do his genius any degree of justice. I read it with disgust; and with a heartfelt sigh, accompanied by a tear, plucked some grass from his grave, which yet remains in my possession. My kind friend politely introduced me to Mrs. Burns, who was pleased to place me

on the chair where the departed favorite of Scotia
sang "his wood notes wild." Her situation seemed
comfortable ; her dress plain, but neat. I wrote a
few lines on visiting the tomb ; but finding it im-
possible to do justice to my feelings, the effusion
was never shewn.

During the many years I spent in Ireland I must
plead guilty to many irregularities of conduct, which
often ended in misery. Every mortal—whether
prince, peer, prelate, or peasant—suffers justly for
indulging in weaknesses ; and these frequently lead
to repentance when too late. Calico printing hav-
ing been on the decline for some years, throughout
Ireland, my return to England became necessary.
On entering Carlisle my surprise at the improvement
made throughout the ancient city was beyond
description. Few persons, on returning to the place
of their nativity, have experienced more kindness ;
not only from the companions of youth or manhood,
but from rich and poor, to me unknown. In con-
sequence of my return a dinner was ordered at the
Grey Goat ; at which a numerous and respectable
party attended. Mr. Henry Pearson, solicitor,
whose humour has amused all classes, was appointed
president ; and the evening was spent in a festive
manner, which afforded a pleasant morning's reflec-
tion.

The many narrow escapes I have had are truly
singular ; one of them may be stated. About the
year 1805, a clergyman, whom I had respected from

my childhood, and would have done anything to serve him, snapped a pistol at my head, across a small table ; without the least provocation.   This happened in Carlisle, in the presence of several persons.

After gleaning so copiously from the bard's auto-biography, it only now remains for the editor to gather up a few fragments which have fallen in his way at intervals.

While the present century was yet young, Anderson's abilities as a versifier were widely known, and in some quarters had become to be much dreaded, as may be gathered from a letter which he addressed to the editor of the *Carlisle Chronicle* in the year 1808 :—

SIR,—The following letter I received yesterday morning. As the production of an *insect* may be amusing to some readers, I wish it to be inserted in your Paper.   Yours, &c.— R. ANDERSON.

CARLISLE, 15 Feb. 1808.

SIR—I understand you are at present employing your vacant hours in composeing a Song, respecting the assembly which was held at Mr. Scarrows, Styled the Butter fly Ball, in hopes to ridicule the characters of those who attended.   I have just sent you these few lines to inform you that if it be the case you will have reason to repent the hour that ever you began it, for if you doo suffer a publication of that description to be made public I can assure you it will be the last you will publish in C[arlisle] or any place else, for you may *depend*

upon it you must not expect to walk the streets of Carlisle un-
protected, therefore I shall leave it to your own judgment to
doo what you think proper.—A FRIEND.

Early in the year 1817, a report got into circulation
that Anderson had been lost in crossing the Irish
channel, on his way to Cumberland to spend the
christmas holidays, which was recorded in the
columns of the *Carlisle Patriot* as follows :—"It is
much to be feared that Mr. Anderson, the ingenious
and well known author of the Cumberland Ballads,
etc., has met with a watery grave. He embarked
at Belfast, about seven weeks ago, in company with
one Robert Peat, a native of this part of the country,
and several others, on board the Catharine of
Maryport, which vessel has not since been heard of.
What tends more strongly to confirm the loss of the
vessel is the fact, that the broken boat of the
Catharine was lately washed on shore at the mouth
of Maryport harbour." In the following number of
the *Patriot* a friend of Anderson's in Belfast, named
Turnbull, writes on his behalf to say that the report
was altogether devoid of truth ; that he took no
passage in any vessel for Cumberland, nor had any
intention of doing so; and that he never was in
better health and spirits than at that time.

Anderson remained in Ireland till the spring of
1819, at which date he returned to his native city,
with the intention of settling there permanently. On
the 24th of March, his fellow citizens entertained
him at the Grey Goat Inn, as is mentioned at the

conclusion of the autobiography. During the following year he issued a miscellaneous collection of his verses in two small volumes, which, (with the exception of a dozen or so of dialect ballads,) is of a very mediocre order.

In 1823, Anderson being much pressed for the want of means, removed to the village of Hayton, near Brampton ; and while living there he offered the copyright of his local ballads for sale, through the medium of the public press, in the following words :—

ROBERT ANDERSON, having revised and altered the CUMBERLAND BALLADS, increased their Number from 75 to 177, added Sixty New Stanzas to the old ones, and prepared a copious Glossary to the whole—offers the Copyright to any Bookseller, inclined to purchase, on reasonable terms. The New Ballads, like the old, are illustrative of Local Feelings, Manners, and Customs, and will not, probably, be found inferior to their successful predecessors.

Letters, Post-paid, addressed to R. ANDERSON, at MR. BROWN'S, Hayton, near Brampton, Cumberland, will be duly attended to.

This appeal was singularly unsuccessful, and failed, I believe, to bring any grist to the mill. No local bookseller, or other person, was found to be venturesome enough to risk the publication of the ballads on the terms proposed by the author. Accordingly, the greater part of the pieces remained in manuscript until an edition—injudiciously edited —was issued by Robertson of Wigton many years after Anderson's death. This collection professes to contain "upwards of one hundred and thirty pieces never before published, besides many additional verses to songs already published"; but being composed of a heterogeneous mass of half digested material, is much more calculated to detract from, than to add to, its author's reputation. It may serve, however, to show the standard of Anderson's culture, when left to work out his own ideas unaided and alone.*

The last years of the bard's life present a sad and mournful chapter in biography. He fell into the vice of intemperance, and by degrees became more and more untidy and careless in his dress. His looks wore a careworn and haggard appearance; and the fear of ending his days in Saint Mary's workhouse haunted his imagination.

> His rest is gone,
> His heart is sore ;
> Peace finds he never
> And nevermore.

He became a thorough misanthropist, not altogether towards mankind, perhaps; but in the full sense of the term, towards dogs and cats and other dumb

---

* By the way, an announcement was made that Anderson's Ballads—two hundred in number—would appear on the 6th of March, 1824, in twenty fortnightly parts, at sixpence each, with a portrait of the author. George Irwin of Carlisle, (the projector of the nondescript *Citizen,* and afterwards editor of the *Whitehaven Herald,*) was advertised as the publisher; but the affair, from some cause or other, seems to have been "nipt i' the bud," for the work was never issued from the press.

animals. A favourite lap-dog, which belonged to a niece of his, had a sorry time of it whenever he visited her house. He was never satisfied until he had either given it a hearty kick with his foot, or a determined pinch with his finger nails ; until at length the poor dog used to make a point of de-camping or hiding itself as soon as he made his appearance.

A weaver, named Jack Lusk, was a boon com-panion of Anderson's during his latter days. Jack was a good singer, and sang several of the Cumber-land ballads in capital style. The two comrades used to meet together at the French Horn public-house, opposite the gaol, kept by one Joe Purdie, a nephew of the bard's. Anderson by times was subject to fits of abstraction, and when these were on he has been known to sit for hours together looking gloomily into the fire, conjuring up all sorts of wild phantasies ; but at other times he was re-markable cheerful and chatty, and would say in a lively tone :—" Come, noo, Lusk, sing us ' Soldier Yeddy' agean, or ' Reed Robin,' or ' The Im-patient Lassie.' "

One who had been his companion for years, and had therefore many opportunities of knowing him thoroughly, once said to me :—" To tak him awtogidder, Anderson wasn't a bad fellow, an' wasn't badly thowt on, owther ; bit as he grew aulder, he sartenly dud grow varra captious an' bad tè du' wi.' If ye happen'd to say to him, ' It's a fine mwornin', Mr Anderson,'—ten-to-yan bit his reply wad be, ' Dust'e tak me for a fool or a bworn idiot ? I kent *that* lang afooar I saw thee !' "

His companion once went with him from Upperby to the Bush hotel in Carlisle, to wait upon a gentleman who admired his ballads, and, knowing his difficulties, was anxious to render him some assistance. When they called at the hotel, the gentleman happened to have gone out a sight-seeing ; being at the cathedral, or castle, or some other place of like interest. In order, therefore, to pass the time till his return, the two friends strolled into Joe Purdie's public-house, where a few glasses of whiskey-toddy were the means of upsetting their project altogether. Through the hilarity of the moment, poor Anderson became quickly transformed, from a state of dependence, into one of absolute *in*dependence. Sitting with difficulty on his chair, he gesticulated wildly, struck his hand repeatedly on the table, and kept repeating :—"I'll nut budge an inch, nut I, for ony gentleman leevin' ! I'll nut be behodden to t' best man i' t' land ! "

Anderson lived and died a bachelor, and finally finished his career in Annetwell-street, Carlisle, on the 26th September, 1833. A monument of white marble, surmounted by a profile in the basso-relievo style, has been erected to his memory in the Cathedral. A memorial stone also marks his grave in the adjoining churchyard of Saint Mary. May the green sod cover lightly his earthly dust !

Anderson commenced his career in times of
comparative primitive simplicity. Our ancestors
had to bear the brunt of many a stout siege and
fierce foray with Scottish moss-troopers and clans-
men ; had to evade and drive back the border-bred
raiders when they swarmed into Cumberland, to
pillage the flocks and herds grazing among the rich
meadows and sunny uplands. With the union of
the two kingdoms, and the memorable 1745, more
peaceful days dawned. The maidens and matrons ·
now sat undisturbed in the ingle-nook, diligently
plying their spinning wheels. Throughout Cumber ·
land and the Lake country, the mode of life was in a
high degree pastoral and primitive. The principal
articles of diet were oatmeal-cake and porridge,
milk, butter, cheese—not including even potatoes.
Tea was almost unknown ; butcher's meat was cooked
but once a year ; and so uncertain and slow in
transmission were the conveyances of these days,
that it was customary for people to make their wills
before going to London.

Anderson's "Ballads in the Cumberland Dialect"
have passed through numerous editions, and still
enjoy a considerable reputation in his native dis-
trict.* He may fairly be called the bard of our
peasantry. There are few ploughmen, shepherds,
or buxom country girls throughout the county, who

*Among the subscribers to the two volume edition of 1820,
it is pleasing to find the names of Robert Southey of Greta
Hall, poet laureate, and William Wordsworth of Rydal
Mount.

are not in some degree acquainted with his ballads.
With many they have long been pocket companions.
He has sung of their love-trystes and adventures ;
has told how long excursions to lonely farm-houses
were braved on stormy nights over hills and moors
and mosses ; how rivals were met and baffled ; how
maidens love to be wooed and won when the moon-
light falls upon quiet glens and nooks of hawthorn.
His descriptions of fairs, "merrie-neets," and other
festive occasions are related in their every-day
language and appeal to their common experience.
There is a happy naturalness of expression about
many of his phrases which causes them to be
continually quoted in our midst ; and so truthfully
daguerreotyped are some of the characters in his
ballads, that we feel as if we had often met them in
our daily intercourse, and could hold converse face
to face with them.

Many of the songs which Anderson has left are
intensely and thoroughly Cumberland songs, and
belong to no other county ; they are Cumberland
in expression, feeling, and sentiment ; they are
Cumberland even in their prejudices and braggings,
for does not

> Canny auld Cummerlan' cap them aw still ?

He has painted a faithful picture of manners and
customs now almost obsolete. In this respect
Anderson has had no rival. His sense of the
ludicrous was keen and piercing. The follies, vices,

and conceits of the peasantry were seized upon with a quick and penetrating glance. The song of the *Ill gien Wife* is one of the best examples of this class. It was a master stroke of satire to compare the wife's " dour and durty smock" to "Auld Nick's nuttin' bag ! " And does not a sense of utter wretchedness overshadow the mind as the poor cuckold of a husband moans out these words ?

> Grin, grinnin'—din, dinnin' !
> Toil and misery !
> Better feed the kurk-yard worms
> Than leeve sec slaves as we.

These four lines are worthy of Burns or Tom Hood, and greater praise cannot be given.

Anderson is inferior to Miss Blamire in force of thought—sharp, clear, original reflection—and in fine poetic feeling ; to Stagg the blind bard of Wigton, in graphic sketches of character and masculine firmness of language. His models have evidently been the fine old love songs of Scotland. It is only at rare intervals, however, that the true spirit is caught, and even then passes hastily away. Often he has left us but faint echoes of these glorious originals. If judged by his compositions in English alone—such as the *Rose of Corby*—he must be pronounced a poor metre-monger. Even his songs in the Cumberland dialect, upon which his reputation is entirely built, possess very unequal merit. Many are of the most commonplace order ; while others are faithfully limned and touched in with the nicety of a Dutch painter. As specimens of his better style I would single out *The Impatient Lassie, Will and Kate, King Roger, Reed Robin, The Bashfu' Wooer, Gwordie Gill, Peggy Pen,* and the *Worton Wedding.* These are songs which any county, within the four seas, might be proud to possess.

Had Anderson aroused himself to a greater earnestness of purpose, and not frittered away his powers by continuous scribbling, he might have attained much greater excellence and fame. As it was, we find that instead of *rising* to the dignity of his subject, he too often *fell* below it. Those who wish well to his name will speak only of his earliest and best productions; and will try to forget the easy-going, jog-trot efforts of his later years, in which he lacks variety of treatment, gets gravelled from want of thought, and falls into a childish strain of moralizing.

In looking around on humanity, the sweep of his mind was narrow and circumscribed. He has merely sketched the eddies floating on the surface, and left the deep undercurrent to roll on undisturbed. Like some of his contemporaries, he has pictured the hardy Cumbrian peasant too exclusively from one point of view and one only; namely, that of an ale-drinking, guzzling, cock-fighting, card-playing animal. The passions, virtues, and struggles of life in its humbler forms, remain untouched : of these he knew little and sung nothing. That there are pure and elevating subjects for poetry

to be found " in huts were poor men lie," no one
can gainsay.   Have not many of our poets given us
bursts of noble and tender feelings which had their
origin in the lowly homes of the people ; as witness
Wordsworth, Hood, Kingsley, and above all Robert
Burns ?   Tried by this standard Anderson's ballads
will certainly be found wanting ; and yet from many
points of view he has left us a great deal that is
valuable.   His pages reflect so much of the peasant's
ordinary every-day life, that country lasses will long
delight to warble his love-songs ; and rustic lads
continue to set the village gathering, seated round
the winter fireside, in roars of laughter with his
humorous ones.

ROBERT ANDERSON'S

CUMBERLAND BALLADS.

REED ROBIN.

[AIR : "Hallow Fair."—"This song," says Anderson, "was occasioned by a redbreast visiting for five years my retired apartments in the centre of Carlisle. He commonly gave me his first cheerful strain in the beginning of September ; and sang his farewell to the noise and smoke of the town in April. So tame was the merry minstrel, that he frequently made a hearty repast within a few inches of the paper on which I wrote."—On one occasion, after a long absence from Carlisle, Anderson wept like a child on casually overhearing some one sing this song in an adjoining room of the Black Swan in Castle Street. Its engaging simplicity is entirely destroyed in a Scotch imitation of it commencing " O where are you going sweet Robin," which will be found in Robert Chambers' *Scottish Songs*, 1829, and in Whitelaw's collection.

COME into my cabin, reed Robin !
   Thrice welcome, blythe warbler, to me !
Now Skiddaw hes thrown his white cap on
   Agean I'll gi'e shelter to thee.
Just hop thy ways into my pantry,
   And feast on my peer humble fare ;
I niver was fash'd wid a dainty,
   But mine, man or burd sal ay share.

Now four years are by-geane, reed Robin,
  Sin furst thou com singin' to me ;
But, oh, how I's chang'd, little Robin,
  Sin furst I bade welcome to thee !
I then hed a bonny bit lassie,
  Away wid anudder she's geane ;
My frien's wad oft caw at my cabin,
  Now dowie I seegh aw my leane.

Oh, where is thy sweetheart, reed Robin ?
  Gae bring her frae house-top or tree ;
I'll bid her be true to sweet Robin,
  For fause was a lassie to me.
You'll share iv'ry crumb i' my cabin,
  We'll sing the cauld winter away ;
I wunnet deceive ye, peer burdies !
  Let mortals use me as they may.

November, 1800.

BETTY BROWN.

AIR : "John Anderson my jo."

WULLY.

Come, Gwordie lad, unyoke the yad,
  Let's gow to Rosley Fair ;
Lang Ned's afwore, wi' Symie' lad,
  Peed Dick, and monie mair :

The Cumberland Bard.

My titty Greace and Jenny Bell
  Are gangen bye and bye,
Sae doff thy clogs, and don thysel—
  Let fadder luik to t' kye.

GWORDIE.

O, Wully ! leetsome may ye be !
  For me, I downa gang ;
I've often shek'd a leg wi' t'ee,
  But now I's aw whyte wrang ;
My stomach's gean, nae sleep I get ;
  At neet I lig me down,
But nobbet pech, and gowl, and fret,
  And aw for Betty Brown.

Sin Cuddy Wulson' murry-neet,
  When Deavie brees'd his shin,
I've niver, niver yence been reet,
  And aw for her I fin' :
T'ou kens we danc'd a threesome reel,
  And Betty set to me—
She luik'd sae nice, and danc'd sae weel,
  What cou'd a body de ?

My fadder fratches sair eneugh,
  If I but steal frae heame ;
My mudder caws me peer dyl'd guff,
  If Betty I but neame :

Atween the twea there's sec a frase,
  O but it's bad to 'bide !
Yet, what's far waur, aye Betty says,
  She wunnet be my bride.

WULLY.

Wey, Gworge ! t'ou's owther fuil or font,
  To think o' sec a frow ;
In aw her flegmagaries donn'd,
  What is she ?—nowte 'at dow ;
There's sceape-greace Ben, the neybors ken,
  Can git her onie day—
Ere I'd be fash'd wi' sec a yen,
  I'd list or rin away !

Wi' aw her trinkums on her back,
  She's fine eneugh for t' squire ;
A sairy wife, I trow, she'd mak,
  'At cudn't muck a byre ;—
But, whisht ! here comes my titty Greace,
  She'll guess what we're about—
To mworn-o'mworn, i' this seame pleace,
  We'll hae the stwory out.

BARBARY BELL.

[AIR : "Cuddle and cuddle us aw thegether."—A Cumbrian peasant pays his addresses to his sweetheart during the silence and solemnity of midnight, when every bosom is at rest, except that of love and sorrow. Anticipating her kindness, he will travel ten or twelve miles, over hills, bogs, moors, and mosses, undiscouraged by the length of the road, the darkness of the night, or the intemperature of the weather.—SANDERSON.]

Oh, but this luive is a serious thing !
It's the beginner o' monie waes ;
And yen hed as gud in a helter swing,
  As luik at a bonny feace now a-days :
Was there iver peer deevil sae fash'd as me !
Nobbet sit your ways still, the truth I's tell,
For I wish I'd been hung on our codlen tree,
  The varra furst time I seed Barbary Bell !

Quite lish, and nit owre thrang wi' wark,
  I went my ways down to Carel fair,
Wi' bran new cwoat, and brave ruffl'd sark,
  And Dicky the shaver put flour i' my hair ;
Our side lads are aw for fun,   .
  Some tuik cyder, and some drank yell ;
Diddlin Deavie he strack up a tune,
  And I caper'd away wi' Barbary Bell.

Says I, " Bab," says I, " we'll de weel eneugh,
  For t'ou can kurn, and darn, and spin ;
I can dyke, men' car'-gear, and hod the pleugh ;
  Sae at Whussenday neist we'll t'warld begin :

I's turn'd a gayshen aw t' neybors say,
 I sit like a sumph, nae mair mysel',
And up or a bed, at heame or away,
 I think o' nowte but Barbary Bell.

Then whea sud steal in but Rob o' the Nuik,
 Dick o' the Style, and twea or three mair :
Suin Barb'ry frae off my knee they tuik,
 " Wey, dang it !" says I, "but this is nit fair !"
Robbie he kick'd up a dust in a crack,
 And sticks and neeves they went pel-mel,
The bottles, forby the clock feace, they brack,
 But fares-t'e-weel, white-fit, Barbary Bell.

'Twas nobbet last week, nae langer syne,
 I whin'd i' the nuik, I can't tell how ;
" Git up," says my fadder, "and sarra the swine !"
 " I's bravely, Bab !" says I, "how's t'ou ?"
Neist mworn to t'cwoals I was fworc'd to gang,
 But cowp'd the cars at Tindel Fell,
For I cruin'd aw the way, as I trotted alang,
 " O that I'd niver kent Barbary Bell !"

That varra seame neet up to Barbary' house,
 When aw t'auld fwok were liggin asleep,
I off wi' my clogs, and as whisht as a mouse,
 Claver'd up to the window, and tuik a peep ;
There whea sud I see, but Watty the laird—
 Od whyte leet on him ! I munnet tell !
But on Setterday neist, if I live and be spar'd
 I'll wear a reed cwoat for Barbary Bell.

THE WORTON WEDDING.

[AIR : "Dainty Davie."—As a pourtrayer of rustic man-
ners—as a relator of homely incident—as a hander down of
ancient customs, and of ways of life fast wearing or worn out
—as an exponent of the feelings, tastes, habits, and language
of the most interesting class in a most interesting district, and
in some other respects, we hold Anderson to be unequalled,
not in Cumberland only, but in England.   As a description
of a long, rapid, and varied succession of scenes—every one a
photograph—occurring at a gathering of country people intent
upon enjoying themselves in their own uncouth roystering
fashion, given in rattling, jingling, regularly irregular rhymes,
with a chorus that is of itself a concentration of uproarious fun
and revelry, we have never read or heard anything like Ander-
son's "Worton Wedding."—A. CRAIG GIBSON.]

O, see a weddin' I've been at !
Deil bin, what cap'rin, feightin, vap'rin' !
Priest and clerk, and aw gat drunk—
Rare deins there were there :
The Thuirsby lads they fit the best ;
The Worton weavers drank the meast ;
But Brough-side lairds bang'd aw the rest
For braggin o' their gear,
And singin'—Whurry whum, whuddle whum,
Whulty whalty, wha-wha-wha,
And derry dum, diddle dum,
Derry eyden dee.

Furst helter skelter frae the kurk ;
Some off like fire, through dub and mire ;
" Deil tek the hindmost !" Meer' lad cries—
Suin head owre heels he flew :

"God speed ye weel !" the priest rwoar'd out,
" Or neet we's hae a hearty bout"—
Peer Meer' lad gat a blacken'd snout—
   He'd mickle cause to rue—
     It spoil'd his—Whurry whum, &c.

When on the teable furst they set
   The butter'd sops,.sec greasy chops,
'Tween lug and laggen ! oh what fun,
   To see them girn and eat !
Then lisping Isbel talk'd sae fine,
'Twas " vathly thockin* thuth to dine ;
Theck grivetht wark ! to eat like thwyne !" ‡
   It meade her sick to se'et ;
     Then we sung—Whurry whum, &c.

Neist stut'rin Cursty, up he ruse,
   Wi' a-a-a, and ba-ba-ba ;
He'd kiss Jen Jakes, for auld lang syne,
   And fearfu' wark meade he :
But Cursty, souple gammerstang !
Ned Wulson brong his lug a whang ;
Then owre he flew, the peets amang,
   And grean'd as he wad dee ;
     But some sang—Whurry whum, &c.

* Vastly shocking.   † Such grevious.   ‡ Swine.

Aunt Ester spoil'd the gurdle ceakes,
  The spice left out, was wrang, nea doubt ;
Tim Trummel tuik nine cups o' tea,
  And fairly capp'd t'em aw :
The kiss went roun' ; but Sally Slee,
When Trummel cleek'd her on his knee,
She dunch'd and punch'd, cried, " Fuil, let be ! "
  Then strack him owre the jaw,
    And we sang—Whurry whum, &c.

Far maist I laugh'd at Grizzy Brown,
  Frae Lunnon town she'd just come down,
In furbelows, and fine silk gown,
  Oh, man, but she was crouse !
Wi' Dick the footman she wad dance,
And "wonder'd people could so prance ;"
Then curtchey'd as they dui in France,
  And pautet like a geuse.
    While aw sang—Whurry whum, &c.

Young Sour-milk Sawney, on the stuil,
  A whornpipe danc'd, and keav'd and pranc'd ;
He slipp'd, and brak his left-leg shin,
  And hirpl'd sair about.
Then cocker Wully lap bawk heet,
And in his clogs top time did beat :
But Tamer, in her stockin' feet,
  She bang'd him out and out,
    And lilted—Whurry whum, &c.

II.   6

Now aw began to talk at yence,
    O' naigs and kye, and wots and rye,
And laugh'd and jwok'd and cough'd and smuik'd,
    And meade a fearfu' reek ;
The form it brack, and down they fell,
Lang Isaac leam'd auld granny Bell ;
They up and drank het suggar'd yell,
    Till monie cudn't speak,
        But some sang—Whurry whum, &c.

The bride she kest up her accounts
    In Rachel's lap, then pou'd her cap ;
The parson' wig stuid aw ajy;
    The clerk sang " Andrew Carr ;"
Blin' Stagg, the fiddler, gat a whack,
The bacon fleek fell on his back,
And neist his fiddle-stick they brack,
    'Twas weel he was nea waur,
        For he sang—Whurry whum, &c.

Now on the midden some were laid,
    Aw havey skavey, and kelavey ;
The clogger and the teaylear fit,
    Peer Snip gat twea black een :
Dick Wawby he began the fray,
But Jemmy Moffat ran away,
And crap owre head amang the hay,
    Fwok say nit varra clean ;
        Then they sang—Whurry whum, &c.

Neist Windy Wull, o' Wample side,
  He bang'd them aw, beath girt and smaw ;
He flang them east, he flang them west,
  And bluidy pates they gat ;
To him they wer' but caff and san' ;
He split the teable wi' his han',
But in the dust wi' dancin' Dan,
  They burnt his Sunday hat ;
    Then aw sang—Whurry whum, &c.

The bride now thowt it time for bed ;
  Her stockin' doff'd, and flang 't quite soft—
It hit Bess Bleane—Wull Webster blush'd,
  And luik'd anudder way :
The lads down frae the loft did steal ;
The parish howdey, Greacy Peel,
She happ'd her up, aw wish'd her weel ;
  Then whop'd to meet neist day,
    And sing her—Whurry whum, &c.

The best on't was, the parson swore
  His wig was lost, a crown it cost,
He belsh'd and hiccupp'd, in and out,
  And said it wasn't fair :
Now day-leet it began to peep,
The bridegroom off to bed did creep,
I trow he waddn't mickle sleep,
  But—whisht ! I'll say nea mair,

Nobbet sing—Whurry whum, whuddle whum,
Whulty, whalty, wha-wha-wha,
And derry dum, diddle dum,
Derry eyden dee.

SALLY GRAY.

Air : "The mucking o' Geordie's byre."

Come, Deavie, I'll tell thee a secret,
But t'ou mun lock't up i' thee breast,
I wadden't for aw Dalston parish
It com to the ears o' the rest ;
Now I'll hod t'ee a bit of a weager,
A groat to thy tuppens I'll lay,
T'ou cannot guess whea I's in luive wi',
And nobbet keep off Sally Gray.

There's Cumwhitton, Cumwhinton, Cumranton,
Cumrangen, Cumrew, and Cumcatch,
And mony mair "cums" i' the county,
But nin wi' Cumdivock can match ;
It's sae nice to luik owre the black pasture,
Wi' the fells abuin aw, far away—
There is nea sec pleace, nit in England,
For there lives the sweet Sally Gray !

I was sebenteen last Collop-Monday,
  And she's just the varra seame yage ;
For ae kiss o' the sweet lips o' Sally,
  I'd freely give up a year's wage ;
For in lang winter neets when she's spinnin',
  And singin' about Jemmy Gay,
I keek by the hay-stack, and lissen,
  For fain wad I see Sally Gray.

Hed t'ou seen her at kurk, man, last Sunday,
  T'ou cudn't hae thowt o' the text ;
But she sat neist to Tom o' the Lonnin,
  T'ou may think that meade me quite vext ;
Then I pass'd her gaun owre the lang meadow,
  Says I, " Here's a canny wet day !"
I wad hae said mair, but how cud I,
  When luikin at sweet Sally Gray !

I caw'd to sup cruds wi' Dick Miller,
  And hear aw his cracks and his jwokes ;
The dumb wife was tellin' their fortunes,
  What ! I mud be like other fwoks !
Wi' chawk, on a pair of auld bellows,
  Twea letters she meade in her way—
S means Sally, the wide warl' owre,
  And G stands for nowte else but Gray.

O was I but lword o' the manor,
  A nabob, or parliament man,
What thousands on thousands I'd gie her,
  Wad she nobbet gie me her han' !

A cwoach and six horses I'd buy her,
  And gar fwok stan' out o' the way,
Then I'd loup up behint like a footman—
  Oh ! the warl' for my sweet Sally Gray !

They may brag o' their fine Carel lasses
  The'r feathers, the'r durtment, and leace;
God help them ! peer death-luikin bodies,
  Widout a bit reed i' the'r feace !
But Sally's just like allyblaster,
  Her cheeks are twea rwose-buds in May—
O lad ! I cud sit here for iver,
  And talk about sweet Sally Gray.

————

WILL AND KATE.

AIR : "John Anderson my jo."

Now, Kate, full forty years hae flown,
  Sin' we met on the green ;
Frae that to this the saut, saut tear,
  Hes oft stuid i' my een :
For when the bairns were some peet-heet,
  T'ou kens I leam'd my knee—
Lal toddlen things, in want o' bread—
  O that went hard wi' me.

Then t'ou wad cry, " Come, Wully, lad,
    Keep up thy heart—ne'er fear !
Our bits o' bairns 'll scraffle up,
    Sae dry that sworry tear.
There's Matt sal be an alderman ;
    A bishop we'll mak Guy ;
Lal Ned sal be a clogger ; and
    Dick maun work for t'ee and I.

Then when our crops were spoil'd wi' rain,
    Sir Jwohn mud hev his rent ;
What cud we de ? nea gear hed we—
    Sae I to jail was sent :
'Twas hard to starve i' sec a pleace,
    Widout a frien' to trust ;
But when I thowt o' thee and bairns,
    My heart was like to brust.

Neist Etty, God was pleas'd to tek,
    What then, we'd seven still ;
But whea kens what may happen ?—suin
    The smaw-pox did for Bill :
I think I see his slee-black een,
    Then he wad chirm and talk,
And say, "Ded, ded ; Mam, mam," and aw,
    Lang, lang ere he cud walk.

At Carel, when, for six pun' ten,
    I selt twea Scotty kye,
They pick'd my pocket i' the thrang,
    And deil a plack hed I ;

"Ne'er ack!" says t'ou, "we'll work for mair,
    It's time eneugh to fret;
A pun' o' sorrow wunnet pay
    Ae single ounce o' debt."

Now, toddlen down the hill o' life,
    Auld yage hes browte content;
And, God be thank'd, our bairns are up,
    And pay Sir Jwohn his rent:
When, side by side aw day we sit
    I often think and grieve,
It's hard that death sud part auld fwok,
    When happy they can leeve.

———

THE IMPATIENT LASSIE.

[AIR : "Low down in the broom."—A copy of this song, slightly altered, is given in Whitelaw's *Book of Scottish Songs,* without any writer's name attached.]

Deuce tek the clock! click-clackin' sae,
    Still in a body's ear;
It tells and tells the time is past,
    When Jwohnie sud been here:
Deuce tek the wheel! 'twill nit rin roun'—
    Nae mair to-neet I'll spin,
But count each minute wi' a seegh,
    Till Jwohnie he steals in.

How nice the spunkey fire it burns,
  For twea to sit beside !
And there's the seat whoar Jwohnie sits,
  And I forgit to chide !
My fadder, tui, he snugly snwores ;
  My mudder fast asleep ;
He promis'd oft ; but, oh ! I fear
  His word he wunnet keep !

What can it be keeps him frae me ?
  The road is nit sae lang,
And sleet and snaw are nowte at aw,
  If fwok were fain to gang !
Some ither lass, wi' bonnier feace,
  Hes catch'd his wicked e'e,
And I'll be pointed at at kurk—
  Nay ! suiner let me dee !

O durst we lasses nobbet gang
  And sweetheart them we like,
I'd rin to thee, my Jwohnie lad,
  Nor stop at bog or dyke ;
But custom's sec a silly thing,
  Men aye mun hae their way,
While mony a bonny lassie sits
  And mourns frae day to day.

But, whisht ! I hear my Jwohnie's fit—
  Aye, that's his varra clog !
He steeks the fa'-yett softly tui—
  O hang that cwoley dog !

Now, hey for seeghs and suggar'd words,
Wi' kisses nit a few—
O but this warl's a paradise,
When lovers they pruive true !

NICHOL THE NEWSMONGER.

Air : "The night before Larry was stretch'd."

Come, Nichol, and gie us thy cracks
I seed t'ee gang down to the smiddy :
I've fodder'd the naigs and the nowt,
And wanted to see thee 'at did ec.
Ay, Andrew, lad ! draw in a stuil,
And gie us a shek o' thy daddle ;
I got aw the news far an nar,
Sae set off as fast's I cud waddle.

In France they've but sworrofu' times,
For Bonnypart's nit as he sud be ;
America's nobbet sae sae ;
And England nit quite as she mud be :
Sad wark there's amang blacks and whites,*
Sec tellin' plain teales to their feaces,
Wi' murders, and wars, and aw that—
But, hod—I forget whoar the pleace is.

* Alluding to the insurrection of the Blacks.

Our parson he gat drunk as muck,
　Then ledder'd aw t' lads round about him ;
They say he is nobbet hawf reet,
　And fwok mud as weel be widout him ;
The yell's to be fourpence a quart—
　Odswinge, lad, there will be rare drinkin' !
Billy Pitt's mad as onie March hare,
　And niver was reet, fwok are thinkin'.

A weddin' we'll hev or it's lang,
　Wi' Bet Brag and lal Tom Tagwally ;
Jack Bunton's far off to the sea—
　It'll e'en be the death of our Sally ;
The clogger hes bowte a new wig ;
　Dalston singers come here agean Sunday ;
Lord Nelson's ta'en three Spanish fleets,
　And the dancin' schuil opens on Monday.

Carel badgers are monstrous sad fwok,
　The silly peer deils how they ring up !
Lal bairns hae got pox frae the kye,*
　And fact'ries, like mushrooms, they spring up ;
If they sud keep their feet for awhile,
　And government nobbet pruive civil,
They'll build up as hee as the muin,
　For Carel's a match for the deevil.

* Cow Pox.

The king's meade a bit of a speech,
    And gentlefwok say it's a topper ;
An alderman deet tudder neet,
    Efter eatin' a turkey to supper ;
Our squire's to be parliament man,
    Mess, lad, but he'll keep them aw busy !
Whea thinks t'ee's come heame i' the cwoach,
    Frae Lunnon, but grater-feac'd Lizzy ?

The cock feights are ninth o' neist month,
    I've twea, nit aw England can bang them ;
In Ireland they're aw up in arms,
    It's whop'd there's nea Frenchmen amang them ;
A boggle's been seen wi' twea heads,
    Lord help us ! ayont Wully Carras,
Wi' girt saucer een, and a tail—
    They dui say 'twas auld Jobby Barras.

The muin was at full this neet week ;
    The weather is turn'd monstrous daggy ;
I' th' loft, just at seven last neet,
    Lal Stephen sweethearted lang Aggy :
There'll be bonny wark bye and bye,
    The truth 'ill be out, there's nea fear on't,
But I niver say nowte, nay, nit I,
    For fear hawf the parish sud hear on't.

Our Tib at the cwose-house hes been,
    She tells us they're aw monstrous murry ;
At Carel the brig's tummel'd down,
    And they tek the fwok owre in a whurry.

I carried our whye to the bull;
They've taen seven spies up at Dover;
My fadder compleens of his hip;
And the Grand Turk hes enter'd Hanover.

Daft Peg gat hersel', man, wi' bairn,
And silly pilgarlic's the fadder;
Lal Sim's geane and swapp'd the black cowt,
And cwoley hes wurried the wedder:
My mudder hes got frostet heels,
And peace is the talk of the nation,
For papers says varra neist week,
There's to be a grand humiliation.*

Aunt Meable hes lost her best sark,
And Cleutie is bleam'd varra mickle;
Nowte's seafe out o' doors now-a-days,
Frae a millstone, e'en down to a sickle;
The clock it strikes eight, I mun heame,
Or I's git a deuce of a fratchin';
When neist we've a few hours to spare,
We'll fin' out what mischief's a-hatchin'.

* Illumination.

THE BUNDLE OF ODDITIES.

AIR : "Fie, let us a' to the bridal."

Sit down, and I'll count owre my sweethearts,
    For, faith, a brave number I've had,
Sin' I furst went to schuil wi' Dick Railton,
    But Dick's in his grave, honest lad !
I mind when he cross'd the deep watter,
    To git me the shilapple' nest,
How he fell owrehead, and I skirl'd sae,
    Then off we ran heame, sair distrest.

Then there was a bit of a teaylear,
    That work'd at our house a heale week,
He was sheap'd aw the warl' like a trippet,
    But niver a word durst he speak ;
I just think I see how he squinted
    At me, when we sat down to meat ;
Owre went his het keale on his blue breeks,
    And deil a bit Snippy cud eat.

At partin' he poud up his spirits,
    Says he, " T'ou hes bodder'd my head,
And it sheks yen to rags and to tatters,
    To sew wi' a lang double thread ;"
Then, in meakin' a cwoat for my fadder,
    (How luive dis the senses deceive !)
Forby usin' marrowless buttons,
    To th' pocket whol he stitch'd a sleeve.

The neist was a Whaker, caw'd Jacob,
    He turn'd up the white o' his een
And talk'd about flesh and the spirit—
    Thowt I, what can Gravity mean?
In dark winter neets, i' the lonnins,
    He'd weade thro' the durt 'buin his knee,
It cuil'd his het heart, silly gander!
    And there let him stowter for me.

A lang blue-lipt chap, like a guide-pwost,
    (Lord help us and keep us frae harm!)
Neist talk't about car'-gear and middens,
    And the reet way to mannish a farm;
'Twas last Leady Fair I leet on him,
    He grummell'd and spent hawf-a-crown—
God bless him! hed he gowd i' gowpens,
    I wadn't hae hed sec a clown.

But stop! there was lal wee deef Dicky,
    Wad dance for a heale winter neet,
And at me aw the time wad keep glowrin'—
    Peer man, he was nobbet hawf reet!
He grew jealous o' reed-headed Ellek,
    Wi' a feace like a full harvest muin;
Sae they fit till they beath gat eneugh on't,
    And I laugh'd at beath when 'twas duin.

There's anudder worth aw put together,
    I cud, if I wad, tell his neame;
He gangs past our house to the market,
    And monie a time he's set me heame;

O wad he but ask me this question—
" Will t'ou be my partner for life ? "
I'd answer without any blushes,
    And aye try to mek a gud wife.

DICK WATTERS.

AIR : "Crowdy."

O, Jenny ! Jenny ! where's t'ou been ?
    Thy fadder is just mad at t'ee ;
He seed somebody i' the croft,
    And gulders as he'd worry me.
O monie are a mudder's whopes,
    And monie are a mudder's fears,
And monie a bitter, bitter pang,
    Beath suin and leate her bosom tears !

We brong thee up, put thee to schuil,
    And clead t'ee weel as peer fwok can ;
We larn'd thee beath to dance and read,
    But now t'ou's crazy for a man.
                    O monie are, &c.

When t'ou was young, and at my knee,
    I dwoated on thee day and neet ;
But now t'ou's rakin', rakin' still,
    And niver, niver i' my seet.
                    O monie are, &c.

T'ou's proud, and past aw gud advice—
   Yen mud as weel speak till a stean;
Still, still thy awn way, reet or wrang—
   Mess, but t'ou 'll rue't when I am geane!
               O monie are, &c.

Dick Watters, I hae tel't thee oft,
   Ne'er means to be a son o' mine;
He seeks thy ruin, sure as deeth,
   Then like Bet Baxter t'ou may whine.
               O monie are, &c.

Thy fadder's comin' frae the croft,
   A bonny hunsup, faith, he'll mek;
Put on thy clogs and auld blue brat—
   Heaste, Jenny! heaste! he lifts the sneck!
               O monie are, &c.

THE LASS ABUIN THIRTY.

AIR: "Jockey's Grey Breeks.."

I've wonder'd sin' I kent mysel',
   What keeps the men-fwok aw frae me;
I's as gud-like as cousin Tib,
   And she can hae her choice o' three:
For me, still moilin by mysel,
   Life's just a bitter widout sweets;
The summer brings nea pleasant days,
   And winter tires wi' lang, lang neets.

II.   7

I hed some whopes o' Wully yence,
    And Wully was the only yen ;
I dreamt and dreamt about him lang,
    But whopes and Wully aw are geane :
A kiss he'd hev, I gev him twee,
    Reet weel I mind, amang the hay ;
Neist time we met, he glump'd and gloom'd,
    And turn'd his head anither way.

A fine pink sash my uncle sent
    Frae Lunnon yence ; about my waist
I wore't and wore't, but deil a lad
    At me or sash a luik e'er cast :
My yellow gown I thowt was sure
    To catch some yen at Carel fair,
But, oh ! fareweel to gown and sash,
    I'll niver, niver wear them mair !

The throssle, when cauld winter's geane,
    Aye in our worchet welcomes spring,—
It mun be luive, did we but ken,
    Gars him aroun' his partner sing ;—
The cock and hen, the duck and drake,
    Nay, e'en the smawest birds that flee,
Ilk thing that lives can git a mate,
    Except sec sworry things as me.

I often think how married fwok
    Mun lead a sweet and happy life ;
The prattlin' bairns rin toddlin' roun',
    And tie the husband to the wife :

Then, oh ! what joy when neet draws on !
    She meets him gangin' frae his wark ;
But nin can tell what cheerfu' cracks
    The tweesome hae lang efter dark.

The wise man leeves nit far frae this,
    I'll hunt him out suin as I can ;
He telt Nan Dobson whee she'd wed,
    And I'm as likely, sure, as Nan ;
But still, still moilin by mysel',
    Life's just a bitter widout sweets ;
The summer brings nea pleasant days,
    And winter tires wi' lang, lang neets !

TOM LINTON.

AIR : "Come under my Plaidie."

Tom Linton was bworn till a brave canny fortune,
    His auld fadder screap'd aw the gear up he cud ;
But Tom, country booby, luik'd owre hee abuin him,
    And mix'd wi' the bad, nor e'er heeded the gud ;
At the town he'd whore, gammle, play hell and the
        deevil,
    He wad hev his caper, nor car'd how it com ;
Then he mud hev his greyhounds, guns, setter, and
        hunter,
    And king o' the cockers they aw cursen'd Tom.

I think I just see how the lads wad flock roun' him,
   And, oh! they were fain to shek Tom by the hand!
Then he'd tell how he fit wi' the barbers and bullies,
   And drank wi' the waiter till nowther cud stan';
His watch he wad show, and his lists o' the horses,
   And pou out a guinea, and offer to lay,
Till our peer country lads grew uneasy and lazy,
   And Tom cud hae coax'd hawf the parish away.

Then he drank wi' the squire, and laugh'd wid his
    worship,
   And talk'd of the duke, and the deevil kens whee;
He gat aw the new-fangled oaths i' the nation,
   And mock'd a peer beggar man wanting an e'e:
His fields they were mortgag'd; about it was
    whisper'd,
   A farmer was robb'd nit owre far frae his house;
At last aw was selt his auld fadder hed toil'd for,
   And silly Tom Linton left not worth a sous.

His fortune aw spent, what! he'd hae the laird's
    dowter,
   But she pack'd him off wid a flee in his ear;
Neist thing, an auld comrade, for money Tom
    borrow'd,
   E'en put him in prison, and bade him lig there:
At last he gat out, efter lang he hed suffer'd,
   And sair hed repented the sad life he'd led;
Widout shoon till his feet, in a soldier's auld jacket,
   He works on the turnpike reet hard for his bread.

Now folly seen into, ragg'd, peer, and down-hearted,
  He toils and he frets, and keen wants daily press;
If cronies ride by, wey, alas! they've forgot him,
  For whee can remember auld friends in distress?
O pity, what pity, that in iv'ry county,
  Sae monie Tom Lintons may always be found!
Deuce tak aw girt nwotions, and whurligig fashions,
  Contentment's a kingdom, aye, aw the warl' round!

THE AUTHOR ON HIMSELF.

AIR: "The Campbells are coming."

O, Eden, wheniver I range thy green banks,
And view aw the scenes o' my infantine pranks,
Where wi' pleasure I spworted ere sorrow began,
I sigh to trace onward frae boy to the man:
To memory dear are the days o' yen's youth,
When, enraptur'd we luik'd at each object wi' truth,
And, like fairies, a thousand wild frolics we play'd;
But manhood hes chang'd what youth fondly
    pourtray'd.

I think o' my playmates, dear imps, I lov'd best!
Now divided like larks efter leavin' the nest!
How we trembled to schuil, and wi' copy and buik,
Oft read our hard fate in the maister's stern luik;

In summer, let lowse, how we brush'd thro' the wood,
And meade seevy caps on the brink o' the flood ;
Or watch'd the seap-bubbles, or ran wi' the kite,
Or launch'd paper navies—how dear the delight !

There was Jock Smith, the boggle,—I mind him
    reet weel,
We twee to Blain's hay-loft together wad steal ;
And of giants, ghosts, witches, and fairies oft read ;
Till sae freeten'd we hardly durst creep off to bed ;
Then, in winter, we'd caw out the lasses to play,
And tell them the muin shone as breet as the day ;
Or scamper, like wild things, at huntin' the hare,
Tig-touch-wood, four corners, or twenty gams mair.

Then my fadder, God bless him! at thirteen oft said,
" My lad, I mun git thee a bit of a trade ;
O cud I afford it, mair larnin thou'd get !"
But peer was my fadder, and I's unlarned yet :
And then my furst sweetheart, an angel was she !
But I only meade luive thro' the tail o' my e'e :
I mind when I met her I panted to speak,
But stuid silent, and blushes spread aw owre my
    cheek.

At last, aw the playthings o' youth laid aside,
Now luive, whope, and fear did my moments divide,
And wi' restless ambition deep sorrow began,
But I sigh to trace onward frae boy to the man :

To memory dear are the days o' yen's youth,
When, enraptur'd, we luik'd at ilk object wi' truth,
And, like fairies, a thousand wild frolics we play'd ;
But manhood hes chang'd what youth fondly
    pourtray'd.

THIS LUIVE SAE BREKS A BODY'S REST.

AIR: "Ettrick Banks."

The muin shone breet at nine last neet,
    When Jemmy Sharp com owre the muir :
Weel did I ken a lover's fit,
    And hard him softly tap the duir ;
My fadder started i' the nuik,
    " Rin, Jenny, see what's that," he said :
I whisper'd, " Jemmy, come to mworn,"
    And then a leame excuse suin meade.

I went to bed, but cudn't sleep,
    This luive sae breks a body's rest ;
The mwornin dawn'd, then up I gat,
    And seegh'd and aye luik'd tow'rds the west ;
But when far off I saw the wood,
    Where he unlock'd his heart to me,
I thowt o' monie a happy hour,
    And then a tear gushed frae my e'e.

To-neet my fadder's far frae heame,
    And wunnet come these three hours yet ;
But, O ! it pours, and I'd be leath
    That Jemmy sud for me git wet !
Yet, if he dis, gud heame-brew'd yell
    Will warm his cheerfu' honest heart ;
Wi' him, my varra life o' life !
    I's fain to meet, but leath to part.

———

AULD MARGET.

Auld Marget in the fauld she sits,
And spins, and sings, and smuiks by fits,
And cries as she had lost her wits—
        " O this weary, weary warl' ! "

Yence Marget was as lish a lass
As e'er in summer trod the grass ;
But fearfu' changes come to pass
        In this weary, weary warl' !

Then, at a murry-neet or fair,
Her beauty meade the young fwok stare ;
Now wrinkl'd is that feace wi' care—
        O this weary, weary warl' !

Yence Marget she hed dowters twee,
And bonnier lasses cudna be ;
Now nowther kith nor kin hes she—
        O this weary, weary warl' !

The eldest wi' a soldier gay,
Ran frae her heame, ae luckless day,
And e'en lies buried far away—
        O this weary, weary warl'!

The youngest she did nowte but whine,
And for the lads wad fret and pine,
Till hurried off by a decline—
        O this weary, weary warl'!

Auld Andrew toil'd reet sair for bread—
Ae neet they fan' him cauld, cauld dead,
Nae wonder that turn'd Marget's head—
        O this weary, weary warl'!

Peer Marget! oft I pity thee,
Wi' care-worn cheek and hollow e'e,
Bow'd down by yage and poverty—
        O this weary, weary warl'!

FIRST LUIVE.

AIR: "Cold and Raw."

It's just three weeks sin Carel fair,
  This sixteenth o' September;
There the furst loff of a sweetheart I gat,
  Sae that day I'll remember.

This luive meks yen stupid—ever sin' syne
   I's thinkin' and thinkin' o' Wully ;
I dung owre the knop, and scawder'd my fit,
   And cut aw my thum' wi' the gully.

O, how he danc'd ! and, O, how he talk'd !
   For my life I cannot forgit him :
He wad hev a kiss—I gev him a slap—
   But if he were here I'd let him.
Says he, "Mally Maudlin, my heart is thine !"
   And he brong sec a seegh I believ'd him :
Thowt I, "Wully Wintrep, thou's welcome to mine,"
   But my head I hung down to deceive him.

Twea yards o' reed ribbon to wear for his seake,
   Forby leather mittens, he bowte me ;
But when we were thinkin' o' nowte but luive,
   My titty, deil bin ! com and sought me :
The deuce tek aw clashes ! off she ran heame,
   And e'en telt my tarn'd auld mudder ;
There's sec a te-dui—but let them fratch on—
   Miss him, I'll ne'er git sec anudder !

Neist Sunday, God wullin ! we promis'd to meet,
   I'll git frae our tweasome a baitin ;
But a lee mun patch up, be't wrang or be't reet,
   For Wully he sha'not stan' waitin' :
The days they seem lang, and lang are the neets,
   And, waes me ! this is but Monday !
I seegh, and I think, and I say to mysel',
   O that to-morrow was Sunday !

LAL STEPHEN.

Air : "Hallow Fair."

Lal Stephen was bworn at Kurkbanton,
  Just five feet three inches was he ;
But at ploughin', or mowin', or shearin',
  His match you but seldom cud see ;
Then at dancin', O he was a capper !
  He'd shuffle and loup till he sweat ;
And for singin' he ne'er hed a marrow,
  I just think I hear his voice yet.

And then wid a sleate and a pencil,
  He capp'd aw our larned young lairds ;
And play'd on twea jew-trumps together,
  And aye com off winner at cards :
At huntin' a brock or an otter,
  At trackin' a foumert or hare,
At pittin a cock or at shootin',
  Nae lad cud wi' Stephen compare.

And then he wad feight like a fury,
  And count fast as hops aw the stars,
And read aw the news i' the paper,
  And talk about weddin's and wars ;
And then he would drink like a Briton,
  And spend the last penny he had,
And aw the peer lasses about him,
  For Stephen were runnin' stark mad.

Our Jenny she writ him a letter,
    And monie a fine thing she said—
But my fadder he just gat a gliff on't,
    And faith a rare durdem he meade ;
Then Debby, that leev'd at Drumleenin,
    She wad hev him aw till hersel',
For ae neet when he stuil owre to see her,
    Wi' sugar she sweeten'd his keale.

Then Judy she darn'd aw his stockin's,
    And Sally she meade him a sark,
And Lizzy, the laird's youngest dowter,
    Kens weel whea she met efter dark.
Aunt Ann, o' the wrang side o' fifty,
    E'en thowt him the flower o' the flock—
Nay, to count yen by yen, aw his sweethearts,
    Wad tek a full hour by the clock.

O ! but I was vext to hear tell on't,
    When Nichol the tidings he browte,
That Stephen was geane for a soldier—
    Our Jenny she gowl'd, ay, like owte :
Sin' that we've nae spwort efter supper,
    We nowther git sang or a crack ;
Our lasses sit bitin' the'r fingers,
    Aw wishin' for Stephen seafe back.

THE BASHFU' WOOER.

AIR : "Daintie Davie."

Whene'er ye come to woo me, Tom,
 Dunnet at the window tap,
 Or cough, or hem, or gie a clap,
 To let my fadder hear, man ;
He's auld and feal'd, and wants his sleep,
Sae by the hallan softly creep,
Ye needn't watch, and glowre, and peep,
 I'll meet ye, niver fear, man :
 If a lassie ye wad win,
  Be cheerfu' iver, bashfu' niver ;
 Ilka Jock may git a Jen,
  If he hes sense to try, man.

Whene'er we at the market meet,
 Dunnet luik like yen hawf daft,
 Or talk about the cauld and heat,
 As ye were weather-wise, man ;
Haud up your head, and bauldly speak,
And keep the blushes frae your cheek,
For he whea hes his teale to seek,
 We lasses aw despise, man :
  If a lassie, &c.

I met ye leately, aw yer leane,
  Ye seemed like yen stown frae the dead,
  Yer teeth e'en chatter'd i' yer head,
    But ne'er a word o' luive, man ;
I spak ; ye luik'd anudder way,
Then trimmel'd as ye'd got a flay,
And owre yer shou'der cried, "Gud day,"
    Nor yence to win me struive, man :
        If a lassie, &c.

My auntie left me threescore pun',
  But deil a yen of aw the men,
  Till then, did bare-legg'd Elcy ken,
    Or care a strae for me, man ;
Now, tiggin at me suin and late,
Their cleekin but the yellow bait ;
Yet, mind me, Tom, I needn't wait,
    When I hae choice o' three, man :
        If a lassie, &c.

There lives a lad owre yonder muir,
He hes nae faut but yen—he's puir ;
  Whene'er we meet, wi' kisses sweet,
    He's like to be my death, man ;
And there's a lad ahint yon trees,
Wad weade for me abuin the knees ;
Sae tell your mind, or, if ye please,
    Nae langer fash us baith, man :
        If a lassie, &c.

January, 1803.

THE AUNTY.

We've roughness amang hands, we've kye i' the byre,
Come live wi' us, lassie, it's aw I desire ;
I'll lig i' the loft, and gie my bed to thee,
Nor sal owte else be wantin' that gudness can gie :
Sin' the last o' thy kin, thy peer aunty we've lost,
Thou frets aw the day, and e'en luiks like a ghost.

I mind, when she sat i' the nuik at her wheel,
How she'd twine the slow thread, and aye counsel
    us weel,
Then oft whisper me, " Thou wad mek a top wife ;
And pray God to see thee weel settl'd in life ; "
Then what brave funny teales she cud tell the neet
    through,
And wad bless the peer fwok, if the stormy win' blew.

That time when we saunter'd owre leat at the town,
'Twas the day, I weel mind, when t'ou gat thy
    chintz gown,
For the watters were up, and pick dark was the neet,
And she lissen'd and cry'd, and thowt aw wasn't
    reet ;
But, oh ! when you met, what a luik did she give !
I can niver forgit her as lang as I live.

How I like thee, dear lassie, thou's oft hard me tell;
Nay, I like thee far better than I like mysel;
And when sorrow forsakes thee, to kurk we'll e'en
    gang,
But t'ou munnet sit pinin' thy leane aw day lang;
Come owre the geate, lassie, my titty sal be
A companion to her that's aye dearest to me.

CROGLIN WATTY.

[AIR: "The lads o' Dunse."—In Cumberland, servants
who are employed in husbandry are seldom engaged for a
longer term than half a year. On the customary days of
hiring, they proceed to the nearest town, and that their
intentions might be known, stand in the market-place with a
sprig or straw in their mouths.—SANDERSON.]

If you ax whoar I come frae, I say the fell-side,
Whoar fadder and mudder, and honest fwok bide;
And my sweetheart, O bless her! she thowt nin
    like me,
For when we shuik han's, the tears gush'd frae
    her e'e :
Says I, " I mun e'en git a spot if I can,
But whativer betide me, I'll think o' thee, Nan !"

Nan was a parfet beauty, wi' twea cheeks like codlin
blossoms; the varra seet on her meade my mouth aw watter.
"Fares-te-weel, Watty!" says she; "t'ou's a wag amang t'
lasses, and I'll see thee nae mair!"—"Nay, dunnet gowl,
Nan!" says I,

" For, mappen, ere lang, I'll be maister mysel';"
Sae we buss'd, and I tuik a last luik at the fell.

On I whussel'd and wonder'd ; my bundle I flung
Owre my shou'der, when Cwoley he efter me sprung,
And howled, silly fellow ! and fawned at my fit,
As if to say—Watty, we munnet part yet !
At Carel I stuid wi' a strea i' my mouth,
And they tuik me, nae doubt, for a promisin' youth.

The wives com roun' me in clusters : "What weage dus
t'e ax, canny lad?" says yen.— "Wey, three pun' and a crown ;
wunnet beate a hair o' my beard." "What can t'e dui?".
says anudder.—"Dui ! wey I can plough, sow, mow, shear,
thresh, dyke, milk, kurn, muck a ·byre, sing a psalm, mend
car'-gear, dance a whornpipe, nick a naig's tail, hunt a brock,
or feight iver a yen o' my weight in aw Croglin parish."

An auld bearded hussy suin caw'd me her man—
But that day, I may say't, aw my sorrows began.

Furst, Cwoley, peer fellow ! they hang'd i' the street,
And skinn'd, God forgie them ! for shoon to their
        feet !
I cry'd, and they caw'd me peer hawf-witted clown,
And banter'd and follow'd me aw up and down :
Neist my deame she e'en starv'd me, that niver
        leev'd weel,—
Her hard words and luiks wad hae freeten'd the deil.

She hed a lang beard, for aw t' warl like a billy gwoat,
wi' a kill-dried frosty fcace ; and then the smawest leg o'
mutton in aw Carel market sarrat the cat, me, and her, for a
weck. The bairns meade sec game on us, and thunder'd at
the rapper, as if to waken a corp ; when I oppen'd the duir,
they threw stour i' my een, and caw'd me daft Watty :

Sae I pack'd up my duds when my quarter was out,
And wi' weage i' my pocket, I saunter'd about.

II.   8

Suin my reet-hand breek pocket they pick'd in a fray,
And wi' fifteen white shillin's they slipt clean away,
Forby my twea letters frae mudder and Nan,
Whoar they said Carel lasses wad Watty trepan :
But 'twad tek a lang day just to tell what I saw—
How I skeap'd frae the gallows, the sowdgers and aw.

Ay ! there were some forgery chaps bad me just sign my
neame. " Nay," says I, " you've gotten a wrang pig by the
lug, for I canno write !" Then a fellow like a lobster, aw
leac'd and feather'd, ax'd me, " Watty, wull t'e list ? thou's
owther be a general or a gomoral."—"Nay, I wunnet—
that's plain : I's content wi' a cwoat o' mudder's spinnin."

Now, wi' twea groats and tuppence, I'll e'en toddle
      heame,
But ne'er be a sowdger while Watty's my neame.

How my mudder 'll gowl, and my fadder 'll stare,
When I tell them peer Cwoley they'll niver see mair,
Then they'll bring me a stuil; as for Nan she'll be
      fain,
When I kiss her, God bless her, agean and agean !
The barn and the byre, and the auld hollow tree,
Will just seem like cronies yen's fidgin' to see.

The sheep 'll nit ken Watty's voice now. The peat-stack
we used to lake roun' 'll be burnt ere this ! As for Nan,
she'll be owther married or broken-hearted : but sud aw be
weel at Croglin, we'll hae feastin', fiddlin', dancin', drinkin',
singin', and smuikin', aye, till aw's blue about us :

Amang aw our neybors sec wonders I'll tell,
But niver mair leave my auld friends or the fell.

JENNY'S COMPLAINT.

Air : " Nancy's to the greenwood gane."

O, Lass! I've fearfu' news to tell !
What thinks te's cum owre Jemmy ?
The sowdgers hev e'en pick'd him up,
    And sent him far, far frae me :
To Carel he set off wi' wheat ;
    Them ill reed-cwoated fellows
Suin wil'd him in—then meade him drunk :
    He'd better geane to th' gallows.

The varra seet o' his cockade
    It set us aw a-crying ;
For me, I fairly fainted twice,
    T'ou may think that was tryin' ;
My fadder wad hae paid the smart,
    And show'd a gowden guinea ;
But, lack-a-day! he'd kiss'd the buik,
    And that 'll e'en kill Jenny.

When Nichol tells about the wars,
    It's waur than deeth to hear him ;
I oft steal out, to hide my tears,
    And cannot, cannot bear him ;
For aye he jibes, and cracks his jwokes,
    And bids me nit forseake him ;
A brigadier, or grenadier,
    He says they're sure to meake him.

If owre the stibble fields I gang,
    I think I see him ploughin',
And iv'ry bit o' bread I eat,
    It seem's o' Jemmy's sowin':
He led the varra cwoals we burn,
    And when the fire I's leetin',
To think the peats were in his hands,
    It set's my heart a beatin'.

What can I de? I nowte can de,
    But whinge and think about him :
For three lang years he follow'd me,
    Now I mun live widout him !
Brek heart, at yence, and then its owre !
    Life's nowte widout yen's dearie,
I'll suin lig in my cauld, cauld grave,
    For, oh ! of life I'm weary !

MATTHEW MACREE.

[AIR : " The wee pickle tow."—Anderson composed this song on a fine summer day in 1803, whilst seated under an apple-tree in the Springfield Bowling green, Carlisle.]

Sin I furst work'd a sampleth at Biddy Forsyth's,
    I ne'er saw the marrow o' Matthew Macree ;
For down his braid back hing his lang yellow locks,
    And he hes a cast wi' his bonny grey e'e :

Then he meks us aw laugh, on the stuil when he
    stands,
And acts like the players and gangs wi' his hands,
And talks sec hard words as nit yen understands—
    O, what a top scholar is Matthew Macree !

'Twas nobbet last Easter his cock wan the main,
    I stuid i' the ring rejoicin' to see ;
The bairns they aw shouted, the lasses were fain,
    And the lads o' their shou'ders bore Matthew
        Macree :
Then at lowpin' he'll gang a full yard owre them aw,
And at rustlin', whilk o' them dare try him a faw ?
And whee is't that aye carries off the foot-baw ?
    But the king of aw Cumberland, Matthew Macree.

That time when he fit full two hours at the fair,
    And lang Jemmy Smith gat a famish black e'e ;
Peer Jemmy I yence thowt wad niver paw mair,
    And I was reet sworry for Matthew Macree :
Then he wad shek the bull-ring, and brag the heale
    town,
And to feight, rin, or russle he put down a crown ;
Saint Gworge, the girt champion, o' fame and
    renown,
    Was nobbet a waffler to Matthew Macree.

On Sundays, in bonny white weastcwoat when
    dress'd,
He sings i' the kurk, what a topper is he!
I hear his strang voice far abuin aw the rest,
    And my heart still beats time to Matthew Macree.
Then his fine eight-page ditties, and garlands sae
    sweet,
They mek us aw merry the lang winter neet,
But, when he's nit amang us, we niver seem reet,
    Sae fond are the lasses o' Matthew Macree.

My fadder he left me a house on the hill,
    And I's git a bit lan' sud my aunty dee,
Then I'll wed bonny Matthew wheniver he will,
    For gear is but trash widout Matthew Macree.
We'll try to show girt fwok content in a cot,
And when in our last heame together we've got,
May our bairns and their neybours oft point to the
    spot
Whoar lig honest Matthew and Jenny Macree.

———

FECKLESS WULLY.

Wee Wully wuns on yonder brow,
    And Wully he hes dowters twee;
But nowte cud feckless Wully dui,
    To git them sweethearts weel to see.

For Meg she luik'd beath reet and left,
  Her e'en they bwor'd a body thro' ;
And Jen was deef, and dum', and daft,
  And deil a yen com there to woo.

The neybors wink'd, the neybors jeer'd,
  The neybors flyr'd at them in scworn,
And monie a wicked trick they play'd
  Peer Meg and Jen, beath neet and mworn.

As Wully went ae day to wark,
  He kick'd a summet wid his shoe ;
And Wully glower'd and Wully girn'd,
  "Guide us !" quoth he, "what hae we now ?"

And Wully cunn'd owre six scwore pun',
  And back he ran wi' nimmle heel,
And aye he owre his shou'der glym'd,
  And thowt he'd dealings wi' the deil.

And Wully's bowte a reet snug house,
  And Wully's bowte a bit o' lan' ;
And Meg and Jen are trig and crouse,
  Sin' he the yellow pwokie fan.

Nae mair the neybors wink and jeer,
  But aw shek han's wi' them, I trow ;
And ilk yen talks o' William's gear,
  For Wully's changed to William now.

And some come east, and some come west,
.And some come monie a mile to woo ;
And Meg luiks straight, and Jen hes sense,
And we aw see what gear 'll dui.

Ye rich fwok aw, ye'll aye dui reet :
Ye peer fwok aw, ye'll aye dui wrang :
Let wise men aw say what they will,
It's money meks the meer to gang.

———

THE BLECKELL MURRY-NEET.

[A Cumbrian MERRY-NIGHT is, as its name imports, a
night appropriated to mirth and festivity. It takes place at
some country alehouse during the holidays of Christmas, a
season in which every Cumbrian peasant refuses to be
governed by the cold and niggardly maxims of economy
and thrift.— SANDERSON.]

Ay, lad ! sec a murry-neet we've hed at Bleckell,
　The sound o' the fiddle yet rings i' my ear ;
Aw reet clipt and heel'd were the lads and the lasses,
　And monie a clever lish hizzy was there :
The bettermer swort sat snug i' the parlour,
　I' th' pantry the sweethearters cutter'd sae soft ;
The dancers they kick'd up a stour i' the kitchen ;
　At lanter the card-lakers sat in the loft.

The clogger o' Dawston's a famish top hero,
    And bangs aw the player-fwok twenty to yen ;
He stamp'd wid his fit, and he shouted and royster'd,
    Till the sweat it ran off at his varra chin en' :
Then he held up ae han' like the spout of a tea-pot,
    And danc'd "Cross the buckle" and "Leather-
        te-patch ;"
When they cry'd "bonny Bell!" he lap up to the
        ceilin,
    And aye crack'd his thoums for a bit of a fratch.

The Hiverby lads at fair drinkin' are sipers ;
    At cockin the Dawstoners niver were bet ;
The Buckabank chaps are reet famish sweethearters,
    Their kisses just sound like the sneck of a yett ;
The lasses o' Bleckell are sae monie angels ;
    The Cummersdale beauties aye glory in fun—
God help the peer fellow that glimes at them dancin',
    He'll steal away heartless as sure as a gun !

The 'bacco was strang, and the yell it was lythey,
    And monie a yen bottom'd a quart like a kurn ;
Daft Fred, i' the nuik, like a hawf-rwoasted deevil,
    Telt sly smutty stwories, and meade them aw gurn,
Then yen sung "Tom Linton," anudder "Dick
        Watters,"
    The auld farmers bragg'd o' their fillies and fwoals,
Wi' jibin', and jwokin', and hotchin', and laughin',
    Till some thowt it time to set off to the cwoals.

But, hod! I forgat—when the clock strack eleben,
 The dubbler was brong in, wi' white bread and
 brown;
The gully was sharp, the girt cheese was a topper,
 And lumps big as lapsteans our lads gobbl'd
 down:
Aye the douse dapper lan'lady cried, " Eat and
 welcome,
 I' God's neame step forret; nay, dunnet be
 bleate!"
Our guts aw weel pang'd, we buck'd up for blin'
 Jenny,
 And neist paid the shot on a girt pewder plate.

Now full to the thropple, wi' head-warks and heart-
 aches,
 Some crap to the clock-kease instead o' the duir;
Then sleepin' and snworin' tuik pleace o' their
 rwoarin';
 And teane abuin tudder they laid on the fluir.
The last o' December, lang, lang we'll remember,
 At five i' the mworn, eighteen hundred and twee:
Here's health and success to the brave Jwohny
 Dawston,
 And monie sec meetings may we leeve to see!

THE THUIRSBY WITCH.

AIR : "O'er Bogie."

There's Harraby and Tarraby,
  And Wigganby beside ;
There's Oughterby and Soughterby,*
  And *bys* beath far and wide ;
Of strappin', sonsy, rwosy queens,
  They aw may brag a few ;
But Thuirsby for a bonny lass,
  Can cap them aw, I trow.

Her mudder sells a swope o' drink,
  It is beath stout and brown,
And Etty is the hinny fowt
  Of aw the country roun' ;
Frae east and west, beath rich and peer,
  A-horse, a-fit, caw in—
For whea can pass sae rare a lass,
  He's owther daft or blin'.

Her een are like twea Cursmas sleas,
  But twice as breet and clear ;
Nae rwose cud iver match her feace,
  That yet grew on a brier ;
At town, kurk, market, dance or fair,
  She meks their hearts aw stoun,
And conquers mair than Bonyparte,
  Whene'er she keeks aroun'.

* Names of Cumberland Villages.

Oft graith'd in aw their kurk-gawn gear,
　Like noble lwords at court,
Our lads slink in, and gaze and grin,
　Nor heed their Sunday spwort ;
If stranger leets, her e'en he meets,
　And fin's he can't tell how ;
To touch the glass her hand hes touch'd
　It sets him in a lowe.

Yence Thuirsby lads were—whea but we ?
　And cud hae bang'd the lave,
But now they hing their lugs and luik
　Like fwok stown frae the grave ;
And what they ail in head or heart
　Nae potticary knows—
The little glancin' Thuirsby Witch,
　She is the varra cause.

Of " Black-ey'd Susan," " Mary Scott,"
　" The lass o' Patie's Mill,"
Of " Barbara Allan," " Sally Grey,"
　" The lass o' Richmond-hill,"
Of " Nancy Dawson," " Molly Mog,"
　Though thousands sing wi' glee,
This village beauty, out and out,
　She bangs them aw to see.

THE PECK O' PUNCH.

[The party here alluded to were our author and a few jovial friends. Archy, to whose comfortable cabin they were invited, is a well-known, industrious, and respectable tradesman—the scourge of pretenders, but the friend of humble merit. He is one of the few who can put Care to the rout, make his friends happy, and keep the table in a roar.—ANDERSON.]

'Twas Rob and Jock, and Hal and Jack,
    And Tom and Ned forby,
Wi' Archy drank a peck o' punch,
    Ae neet when they were dry ;
And aye they jwok'd, and laugh'd, and smuik'd,
    And sang wi' heartfelt glee,
" To-neet we're yen, to-morrow geane,
    Syne let us merry be !"

Saint Mary's muckle clock bumm'd eight,
    When each popp'd in his head ;
But ere they rose, they'd fairly drank
    The sheame-feac'd muin to bed ;
            And aye they jwok'd, &c.

To monie a bonnie Carel lass,
    The fairest o' the town,
And monie a manly British chiel,
    The noggin glass went roun' ;
            And aye they jwok'd, &c.

A neybor's fauts they ne'er turn'd owre,
    Nor yence conceal'd their ain—
Had Care keek'd in, wi' wae-worn feace,
    They'd kick'd him out again ;
                For aye they jowk'd, &c.

The daily toil, the hunter's spoil,
    The faithless foreign pow'rs,
The Consul's fate, his o'ergrown state,
    By turns beguil'd the hours ;
                And aye they laugh'd, &c.

Let others cringe, and bow the head,
    A purse-proud sumph to please ;
Fate grant to me aye liberty
    To mix with souls like these ;
Then oft we'll jwoke, and laugh and smuik,
    And sing wi' heartfelt glee,
" To neet we're yen, to-morrow geane,
    Syne let us merry be !"

THE VILLAGE GANG.

"AIR: "Jenny dang the weaver."

There's see a gang in our town,
    The deevil cannot wrang them,
And cud yen get t'em put in prent,
    Aw England cuddent bang them ;

Our dogs e'en bite aw decent fwok,
  Our varra naigs they kick them,
And if they nobbet ax their way,
  Our lads set on and lick them.

Furst wi' Dick Wiggem we'll begin,
  The tiny, greasy wobster;
He's got a gob frae lug to lug,
  And neb like onic lobster.
Dick's wife, they say, was Bran'ton bred,
  Her mudder was a howdey,
And when peer Dick's thrang on the luim,
  She's off to Jwohnie Gowdy.

But as for Jwohnie, silly man,
  He threeps about the nation,
And talks o' stocks and Charley Fox,
  And meakes a blusteration;
He reads the papers yence a week,
  The auld fwok geape and wonder—
Were Jwohnie king, we'd aw be rich,
  And France mud e'en knock under.

Lang Peel the laird's a dispert chap,
  His wife's a famous fratcher,
She brays the lasses, starves the lads,
  Nae bandylan can match her;
We aw ken how they gat their gear,
  But that's a fearfu' stwory,
And sud he hing on Carel Sands,
  Nit yen wad e'er be sworry.

Beane-breaker Jwohn we weel may neame,
 He's tired o' wark, confound him !
By manglin' limbs, and streenin' joints,
 He's meade aw cripples round him :
Mair hurt he's duin than onie yen
 That iver sceap'd a helter ;
When sec-like guffs leame decent fwok,
 It's time some laws sud alter.

The schuilmaister's a conjuror,
 For when our lads are drinkin',
Aw maks o' tricks he'll dui wi' cards,
 And tell fwok what they're thinkin';
He'll glowre at maps, and spell hard words,
 For hours and hours together,
And in the muin he kens what's doin'—
 Nay he can coin the weather !

Then there's the blacksmith wi' ae e'e,
 And his hawf-witted mudder,
'Twad mek a dead man laugh to see
 Them glyme at yen anudder ;
A three-quart piggen full o' keale,
 He'll sup, the greedy sinner,
Then eat a cow'd-lword like his head,
 Ay, onie day at dinner.

Jack Mar, the hirplin piper's son,
 Can bang them aw at leein' ;
He'll breck a lock, or steal a cock,
 Wi' onie yen in bein':

He eats gud meat, and drinks strang drink,
    And gangs weel-graith'd o' Sunday,
And weel he may, a bonnie fray
    Com out last Whissen-Monday.

The doctor he's a parfet pleague,
    And hawf the parish puzzens ;
The lawyer sets fwok by the lugs,
    And cheats them neist by duzzens ;
The parson swears a bonnie stick
    Amang our sackless asses ;
The 'squire's ruin'd scwores and scwores
    O' canny country lasses.

There's twenty mair, coarse as neck-beef,
    If yen hed time to neame them ;
Left-handed Sim, slape-finger'd Sam,
    Nae law cud iver teame them ;
There's blue-nebb'd Watt, and ewe-chinn'd Dick,
    Weel wordy o' the gallows—
O happy is the country side
    That's free frae sec like fellows !

DICKY GLENDININ'.

AIR : "As Patie cam up frae the glen."

My fadder was down at the mill,
My mudder was out wid her spinnin',
When whea sud slip whietly in,
But canny lal Dicky Glendinin';
He poud off his muckle top cwoat,
And drew in a stuil by the hallen,
Then fworc'd me to sit on his knee,
And suin a sad teale began tellin'.

"O Jenny! O Jenny!" says he,
" My likin' for t'ee I can't smudder;
It meade me as sick as a peat,
To think t'ou'd teane up wid anudder;
What! there's been a bonny te-dui
About a lang hulk of a miller!
He's wide-gobb'd and ill-natured tui,
But ae word says aw—he hes siller.

" The lasses aye flyre and mak gam',
And ax me what's got Jenny Forster (
The lads, when we meet i' the lwones,
Cry out, 'Sairy Dick! what t'ou's lost her!'
When Rowley, the miller, last neet
I met, as we com in frae shearin',
Hed the sickle but been our lang gun,
I'd shot him, ay, dead as a herrin.

The Cumberland Bard.

"O! hes t'e forgitten the time,
   T'ou said t'ou lik'd me best of onie ?
And hes t'e forgitten the time,
   T'ou said luive was better than money ?
And hes t'e forgitten the time,
   I mark'd our twea neames on a shillin' ?
T'ou promised to wear't neist thy heart,
   And then to wed me t'ou was willin'.

" The furst time you're cried i' the kurk,
   I'll step my ways up and forbid it ;
When cauld i' my coffin, they'll say,
   'Twas e'en Jenny Forster that did it !
My ghost, the lang neet, aw in white,
   Will shek thee, and gar thee aw shiver—
O the tears how they hop owre my cheeks,
   To think I sud lwose thee for iver !"

"O Dicky ! O Dicky !" says I,
   " I nowther heed house, land, or siller ;
T'ou's twenty times dearer to me,
   Than onie lang hulk of a miller !"
A match we struck up in a crack,
   And Dicky gat sticks and gat beddin' ;
My fadder and mudder are fain—
   Then hey for a gud merry weddin' !

December 10, 1803.

GRIZZY.

AIR : "My auld guidman."

The witch wife begg'd in our backside,
    But went unsarra'd away i' th' pet ;
Our Ester kurn'd as e'er she kurn'd,
    But butter the deuce a crum cud get.
The pez-stack fell and crush'd my fadder ;
    My mudder cowp'd owre, and leam'd hersel' ;
Neist, war and war, what dud we see,
    But Jenny' pet lam' drown'd i' the well.

Auld Grizzy the witch, as some fwok say,
    Meks paddock-rud ointment for sair een,
And cures the tuith-wark wi' a charm,
    Of hard word's neane ken what they mean.
She milks the kye, the urchin's bleam'd ;
    She bleets the kworn wi' her bad e'e ;
When cross'd by lasses, they pruive wi' bairn,
    And if she grummel, they're seafe o' twee.

I yence sweethearted Madge o' th' Mill,
    And whea sae thick as she and I ;
Auld Whang he promis'd tweescore pun',
    A weel-theek'd house, and bit of a stye ;
Ae neet we met at our croft head,
    But Grizzy was daund'rin' aw her leane,
And scarce a week o' days were owre,
    Till Madge to kurk Wull Weer hed teane.

When deef Dick Maudlin lost his wife,
　And said 'twas weel it was nae war ;
When Jerry' black filly pick'd the fwoal,　·
　And hawf-blin' Calep fell owre the scar ;
When mantin Marget brunt her rock ;
　When smuggler Mat was lost i' the snaw ;
When wheezlin' Wully was set i' the stocks ;
　Auld Grizzy aye gat the weyte of aw.

Her feace is like the stump of a yek ;
　She stoops and stowters, sheks and walks ;
Bleer-c'ed and tuithless, wi' a beard ;
　She coughs and granes, and mumps and talks ;
She lives in a shill-house, burns dried sticks,
　And there hes dealins wi' the de'il.
O war she whietly in her grave !
　For where she bides few can dui weel.

———

GWORDIE GILL.

AIR : " Andrew wi' his cutty gun."

Of aw the lads I see or ken,
　There's yen I like abuin the rest ;
He's nicer in his war-day duds,—
　Than others donn'd in aw their best.

A body's heart's a body's awn,
　And they may gie't to whea they will ;
Hed I got ten whoar I hae neane,
　I'd gie them aw to Gwordie Gill.

Whea was't that brack our landlword' garth
　For me, when bairns we went to schuil ?
Whea was't durst venture mid-thie deep,
　To git my clog out o' the puil ?
And when the filly flang me off,
　And lang and lang I laid sae ill,
Whea was't gowl'd owre me day and neet,
　And wish'd me weel?　'Twas Gwordie Gill.

Oft mounted on his lang-tail'd naig,
　Wi' fine new buits up till his knee,
The laird's daft son leets i' the faul,
　And keaves as he wad wurry me ;
Tho' fadder, mudder, uncle, tui,
　To wed this maz'lin tease me still,
I hear of aw his land and brass,
　But oft steal out to Gwordie Gill.

Frae Carel cousin Fanny com,
　And brong her whey-feac'd sweetheart down.
Wi' sark-neck stuck abuin his lugs,
　A peer clipt dinment frae the town :
He minc'd and talk'd, and skipp't and walk'd,
　But tir'd a-gangin up the hill,
And luik'd as pale as ony corp,
　Compar'd to rwosie Gwordie Gill.

My Gwordie's whussle weel I ken,
Lang ere we meet, the darkest neet;
And when he lilts and sings "Skewball,"
Nit playhouse music's hawf sae sweet.
A body's heart's a body's awn,
And they may gie't to whea they will;
I yence had yen, now I hae neane,
For it belangs to Gwordie Gill.

February, 1804.

————

A WIFE FOR WULLY MILLER.

AIR : " Maggie Lauder."

Hout, Wully, lad ! cock up thy head,
Nor fash thysel about her;
Nowte comes o' nowte, sae tek nae thowt,
T'ou's better far widout her.
Peer man ! her fadder weel we ken,
He's but an ass-buird meaker;
But she's town-bred, and, silly gowk,
Thou'd gie thy teeth to teake her.

I've seen thee flyre and jwoke like mad,
At aw our country fellows;
But now thou seeghs and luiks like death,
Or yen gawn to the gallows;

Thou's sous'd owre head and ears i' luive—
Nay, nobbet luik at cwoley !
He wags his tail, as if to say,
    " Wey, what's the matter, Wully ?"

There's lads but few in our town,
    And lasses wanters plenty,
And he that fain wad wed a wife
    May weale yen out o' twenty !—
There's Tamer Toppin, Aggy Sharp,
    And clogger Wilkin' Tibby :—
There's Greacy Gurvin, Matty Meer,
    And thingumbob's lal Debby :

Then there's Wully Guffy' dowter Nan
    At thee aye kecks and glances,
For t'ou's the apple o' her e'en
    At cardin' neets and dances ;
My titty, tui, ae neet asleep,
    Cried, " Canny Wully Miller !"
I poud her hair, she blush'd rwose reed,
    Sae gang thy ways e'en till her.

Tell mudder aw the news t'ou kens ;
    To fadder talk o' the weather ;
Then lilt t'em up a sang or twea,
    To please t'em aw together ;
She'll set thee out, then speak thy mind—
    She'll suit thee till a shavin' ;
But town-bred deames, to sec as we,
    Are seldom worth the havin'.

UNCLE WULLY.

Air: "Woo'd and married an' a'."

"It's a comical warl' this we live in,"
    Says Calep, and Calep says reet ;
For Matty, that's got aw the money,
    Hes e'en geane and wedded deyl'd Peat.
He's nobbet a heather-feac'd maz'lin,
    And disn't ken whisky frae yell ;
But her, weel brong up and a scholar,
    Hes just meade a fuil o' hersel' !
De'il bin but she'd little to de,
To tek sec a hawflin as he,
That nowther kens A, B, nor C !—
Nay, what sec a pair can ne'er 'gree !

He ne'er hes a teale widout laitin,
    And hardleys can grease his awn clogs ;
He marry a decent man's dowter !
    He's fitter to lig amang hogs !
At the clock for an hour he'll keep glymin',
    But de'il e'er the time he can tell ;
And my niece, for that ae word husband,
    Hes e'en geane and ruin'd hersel.
                    De'il bin, &c.

Her fadder, God keep him ! my billy,
    Aye thowt her the flow'r o' them aw ;
And said on his deeth-bed, "O, Wully !
    Luik till her man ! when I lig low !"

I meade her beath reader and writer—
Nin bang'd her, the maister can tell ;—
But, spite o' beath larnin' and manners,
She's e'en meade a guff of hersel.
                              De'il bin, &c.

When lasses git past aw advisin',
   Our's then turns a piteous case ;
A cwoat or sark yen may shep them,
   But aw cannot gie them God's grace :
For me, I'll e'en deet my hands on her,
   And this aw our neybors I'll tell ;
She's meade a bad bed, let her lig on't,
   And think how she's ruin'd hersel.
De'il bin but she'd little to de,
To tek sec a mazlin as he,
That nowther kens A, B, nor C !—
Nay, what sec a pair can ne'er 'gree !

GUD STRANG YELL.

Our Ellek likes fat bacon weel,
   And haver-bannock pleases Dick ;
A cowd-lword meks lal Wully fain,
   And cabbish aye turns Phillip sick ;

Our deame's for gurdle-keake and tea,
  And Betty's aw for thick pez-keale ;
Let ilk yen fancy what they wull,
  Still my delight is good strang yell.

I ne'er had muckle, ne'er kent want,
  Ne'er wrang'd a neybor, frien', or kin ;
My wife and bairns 'buin aw I prize—
  There's music i' their varra din :
I labour suin, I labour leate,
  And chearfu' eat my humble meal ;
My weage can feed and clead us aw,
  And whiles affords me good strang yell.

What's aw the warl' widout content?
  Wi' that and health man can't be peer ;
We suin slip off frae frien's and foes,
  Then whea but fuils wad feight for gear ;
'Bout kings and consuls gowks may fratch ;
  For me I scworn to vex mysel,
But laugh at courts and owre-grown knaves,
  When I've a hush o' good strang yell.

BURGH RACES.

[The races celebrated in this ballad took place on the 3rd of May, 1804, at Burgh, a village in the neighbourhood of Carlisle, where the warlike Edward died on an expedition that was to decide the fate of Scotland. These races are only held when the heir to the Lowther estates comes into the possession of his lordly domains. Since 1804 races have been celebrated there in 1845 and 1873.]

O Wully ! hed t'ou nobbet been at Burgh Races !
    It seem'd, lad, as if aw the warl' was met ;
Some went to be seen, others off for divarsion,
    And monie went there a lock money to bet ;
There was " How fens t'e, Tommy ? "—What,
        Jwosep ! I's gaily :
Wey, is there owte unket i' your country side ?
Here, landlword, a noggin ! "—" Whea rides the
        Collector ? "
    " What, Meason' auld meer can bang aw far and
        wide ! "

Ere they saddl'd, the gam'lers peep'd sair at the
        horses ;
    See scrudgin', the fwok were just ready to burst ;
Wi' swearin' and bettin' they meade a sad hay-bay :
    " I'll lig six to four ! "—" Done ! come, down wi'
        the dust ! "

"What think ye o' Lawson ?"—"The field for a
  guinea !"
" I'll mention the winner ! dare onie yen lay ?"
Jwohn Blaylock' reed handkitcher wav'd at the
  dissnens :
At startin he cried, " Yen, twee, three, put away !"

They went off like leetnin'—the auld meer's a
  topper—
She flew like an arrow, and shew'd t'em her tail :
They hugg'd, whupp'd, and spurr'd, but cud niver
  yence touch her—
The winners they rear'd, and the lwosers turn'd
  pale ;
Peer Lawson gat dissen'd, and sae sud the tudders,
  Furst heat was a chase, and the neist a tek-in ;
Then some drank their winnins ; but, woefu'
  disaster,
It rain'd, and the lasses gat wet to the skin.

Like pez in a pot, neist at Sandsfield they caper'd,
  The lads did the lasses sae kittle and hug ;
Young Crosset, i' fettle, hed got bran new pumps on,
  And brong fisher Jemmy a clink i' the lug ;
The lasses they belder'd out, "Man thysel, Jemmy !"
  His comrades they poud off his cwoat and his
  sark ;
They fit, lugg'd and lurry'd, aw owre blood and
  batter,
  The lan'lword com in, and cried, " Shem o' sec
  wark !"

There were smugglers, excisemen, horse-cowpers,
    and parsons,
Sat higglety-pigglety, aw fare alike ;
And mowdy-warp Jacky—ay, man, it was funny!—
    He meade them aw laugh, when he stuck in a
    cryke.
There were lasses frae Wigton, and Worton, and
    Ban'ton—
    Some o' them gat sweethearts, while others gat
    neane :
And bairns yet unbworn 'll oft hear o' Burgh Races,
    For ne'er mun we see sec a meetin' agean.

NED CARNAUGHAN.

AIR : "The Miller of Dee."

My mudder was takin her nuin's rest,
    My fadder was out at the hay,
When Ned Carnaughan com bouncin' in,
    And luik'd as he'd gotten a flay :
"O, Sib !" says he, " I's duin wi' t'e ;—
    Nay, what, t'ou blushes and stares !—
I seed thee last neet wi' bow-hough'd Peat,
    And de'il tek them that cares !"

Says I to Ned, to Ned says I,
 " What's aw this fuss about ?
I's seer he's a reet lish country lad,
 And t'ou's just a parfet lout :
But whea were liggen i' Barney's croft,
 And lakin like twea hares ?
And whea kiss'd Suke frae lug to lug ?
 Wey, de'il tek them that cares !"

Says Ned, says he, " The thimmel gie me
 I brong thee frae Bran'ton fair,
And gie back the broach and true-love knot,
 And lock o' my awn reed hair ;
And pay me the tuppence I wan frae thee
 Ae neet at pops and pairs ;
Then e'en tek on wi' whea thou likes—
 The de'il tek them that cares !"

The broach and thimmel I flang at his feace,
 The true-love knot i' the fire ;
Says I, " T'ou's nobbet a hawflin bworn—
 Fash me nae mair, I desire ;—
Here, tek thy tuppence, a reape to buy,
 And gi'e thysel nae mair airs ;
But hing as hee as Gilderoy—
 The de'il tek them that cares !"

Then Ned he trimmelt, and seegh't, and gowlt ;
 I fan' mysel' aw whyte queer :
"O, Sibby !" say he, " my fauts forgie !
 I'll wrang the' nea mair, I swear !"

He kiss'd and coddel't, and meade me smile—
We meet at markets and fairs,
His bride I'll be—sud we ne'er 'gree,
Wey—De'il tek them that cares !

CANNY CUMMERLAN'.

Air : "The humours of glen."

'Twas ae neet last week, wi' our wark efter supper,
We went owre the geate cousin Isbel to see ;
There was Sibby frae Curthet, and lal Betty Byers,
Deef Debby, forby Bella Bunton and me ;
We'd scarce begun spinnin', when Sib a sang lilted,
She'd brong her frae Carel by their sarvant man ;
'Twas aw about Cummerlan' fwok and fine pleaces ;
And, if I can think on't ye's hear how it ran.

Yer buik-larn'd wise gentry, that's seen monie
    counties,
May preach and palaver, and brag as they will
O' mountains, lakes, valleys, woods, watters, and
    meadows,
But canny auld Cummerlan' caps them aw still :

It's true we've nea palaces shinin' amang us,
  Nor tall marble towers to catch the weak eye ;
But we've monie fine castles, whoar fit our brave
    fadders,
  When Cummerlan' cud any county defy.

Furst Graystock we'll nwotish, the seat o' girt Norfolk,
  A neame still to freemen and Englishmen dear ;
Ye Cummerlan' fwok, may your sons and your
    grandsons
  Sec rare honest statesmen for iver revere ;
Corruption's a sink that 'll puzzen the country,
  And lead us to slav'ry, to me it seems plain ;
But he that hes courage to stem the black torrent,
  True Britons sud pray for agean and agean.

Whea that hes climb'd Skiddaw, hes seen sec a
    prospect,
  Whoar fells frown owre fells, and in majesty vie ?
Whea that hes seen Keswick, can count hawf its
    beauties,
  May e'en try to count hawf the stars i' the sky :
There's Ullswater, Bassenthwaite, Westwater, Der-
    went,
  That thousands on thousands hae travell'd to view,
The langer they gaze, still the mair they may wonder,
  And aye, as they wonder, may fin' summet new.

II.   10

We've Corby, for rocks, caves, and walks, sae
    delightfu',
That Eden a paradise loudly proclaims ;
O that sec like pleaces hed aye sec like awners,
    Then mud monie girt fwok be proud o' their neames !
We've Netherby, tui, the grand pride o' the border,
    And haws out o' number nae county can bang ;
Wi' rivers romantic as Tay, Tweed, or Yarrow,
    And green woodbine bowers weel wordy a sang.

We help yen anudder ; we welcome the stranger ;
    Oursels and our country we'll iver defend ;
We pay bits o' taxes as weel as we're yable,
    And pray, like true Britons, the war hed an end ;
Then, Cummerlan' lads, and ye lish rwosy lasses,
    If some caw ye clownish, ye needn't think sheame ;
Be merry and wise, enjoy innocent pleasures,
    And aye seek for health and contentment at
    heame.

TIB AND HER MAISTER.

I's tir'd wi' liggin' aye my leane ;
    This day seems fair and clear ;
Seek th' auld grey yad, clap on the pad,
    She's duin nae wark te year :

Furst, Tib, git me my best lin sark,
  My whig, and new-greas'd shoon ;
My three-nuik'd hat, and mittens white—
  I'll hev a young wife suin !
    A young wife for me, Tib,
    A young wife for me ;
    She'll scart my back whene'er it yucks,
    Sae married I mun be !

" Wey, maister ! you're hawf blin' and deef—
  The rain comes pourin' down :—
Your best lin sark wants beath the laps
  Your three-nuik'd hat the crown ;
The rattens eat your clouted shoon ;
  The yad's unshod and leame ;
You're bent wi' yage like onie bow,
  Sae sit content at heame !
    A young wife for ye, man !
    A young wife for ye !
    They'll rank ye wi' the horned nowt
    Until the day ye dee !"

O, Tib, thou aye talks like a fuil !
  I's fail'd, but nit sae auld ;
A young wife keeps yen warm i' bed,
  When neets are lang and cauld :
I've brass far mair than I can count,
  And sheep, and naigs, and kye,
A house luiks howe widout a wife—
  My luck I'll e'en gae try.

A young wife for me, Tib,
A young wife for me;
I yet can lift twea pecks o' wots,
Tho' turn'd o' eighty-three.

"Weel, maister, ye maun hae your way,
And sin ye'll wedded be,
I's lish and young, and stout and strang.
Sae what think ye o' me ?
I'll keep ye tidy, warm, and clean,
To wrang ye I wad scworn."
Tib ! gie's thy hand !—a bargain be't—
We'll off to kurk to-mworn !
A young wife for me, Tib,
T'ou was meade for me ;
We'll kiss and coddle aw the neet,
And aye we'll happy be !

THE CLAY DAUBIN.

[AIR : "Andrew Carr."—In the eastern and northern parts of Cumberland, the walls of houses are in general com-posed of clay, and in their erection take seldom more than the space of a day.   When a young rustic marries, the highest ambition of his heart is to be the master of an humble clay-built cottage, that might afford shelter to him and his family. As soon as he has selected a proper site, he signifies his intentions to his neighbours, who punctually muster on the spot where the intended building is to be raised, each indivi-dual bringing a spade and one day's provisions along with him. -SANDERSON.]

We went owre to Deavie's Clay Daubin,
  And faith a rare caper we had,
Wi' eatin', and drinkin', and dancin',
  And rwoarin', and singin', like mad ;
Wi' crackin', and jwokin', and braggin',
  And fratchin', and feightin', and aw,
Sec glorious fun and divarsion
  Was ne'er seen in castle or ha'.
    Sing hey for a snug clay biggin,
      And lasses that like a bit spwort ;
    Wi' friends and plenty to gie them,
      We'll laugh at King Gworge and his court.

The waws were aw finish'd er darknin ;
  Now, grypes, shouls, and barrows thrown by,
Auld Davie spak up wid a hursle—
  " Od rabbit it lads, ye'll be dry ;
See deame, if we've got a swope whusky—
  I's sworry the rum bottle's duin—
We'll starken our kites, I'll uphod us—
  Come, Adams,* rasp up a lal tune !"

When Bill kittl'd up " Chips and Shavin's,"
  Auld Philip pou'd out Matty Meer,
Then nattled his heels like a youngen,
  And caper'd about the clay fleer ;

---

* William Adams was an excellent country musician, par-
ticularly noted for playing jigs and strathspeys ; a man well
known at fairs, merry-nights, kurn-suppers, and clay-daubins.

He deeted his gob, and he buss'd her,
　As lish as a lad o' sixteen ;
Cries Wull, " Od dy ! fadder's i' fettle !
　His marrow 'll never be seen !"

Reet sair did we miss Jemmy Coupland—
　Bad crops, silly man, meade him feale ;
Last Sunday forenuin, efter sarvice,
　I' th' kurk-garth, the clerk caw'd his seale.*
Peer Jemmy ! of aw his bit oddments
　A shottle the bealies hae ta'en,
And now he's reet fain of a darrak,
　For pan, dish, or spuin he hes neane.

Wi' scons, *leather-hungry*,† and whusky,
　Auld Aggy cried, " Meake way for me !
Ye men fwok eat, drink, and be murry,
　While we i' the bower git tea."
The whillymer ate teugh and teasty,
　Aw cramm'd fou o' grey pez and seeds ;
They row'd it up teane agean tudder—
　Nae dainties the hungry man needs.

* The "kurk-garth" or church-yard on a Sunday morning used to be to the country people of Cumberland what the Exchange is to the merchants of London. It answered all the purposes of business or amusement, from whence general information was sent round the parish.

† This is a ludicrous name given to a poor sort of cheese made of skimmed milk. It is also called Whillymer, and sometimes Rosley Cheshire.

Now in com the women frok buncin'—
  Widout t'em there's niver nae fun ;
Wi' whusky aw weeted their wizzens,
  But suin a sad hay-bay begun ;
For Jock, the young laird, was new wedded,
  His auld sweetheart, Jenny, look'd wae ;
While some were aw titterin and flyrin,
  The lads rubb'd her down wi' pez strae.*

Rob Lowson tuik part wi' peer Jenny,
  And brong snift'rin' Gwordie a cluff ;
I' th' scufile they leam'd Lowson' mudder,
  And fain they'd hae stripp'd into buff :
Neist Peter caw'd Gibby a rebel,
  And aw rwoar'd out, that was whyte wrang ;
Cried Deavie, "Shek han's, and nae mair on't—
  I's sing ye a bit of a sang."

He lilted "The King and the Tinker,"
  And Wully struck up "Robin Hood ;"
Dick Mingins tried "Hooly and Fairly,"
  And Martha "The Babs o' the Wood ;"
They push'd round a glass like a noggin,
  And bottom'd the greybeard complete ;
Then crack'd till the muin glowr'd amang them,
  And wish'd yen anudder gud neet.

* Formerly a Cumbrian girl, when her lover proved
unfaithful to her, was by way of consolation rubbed with
pease-straw by the neighbouring lads ; and when a youth
lost his sweetheart, by her marriage with a rival, the same
sort of comfort was administered to him by the lasses of the
village.

THE FELLOWS ROUND TORKIN.

[AIR : "The Yorkshire Concert."—Torkin is ,a wood-covered hill, near Crofton-hall, the seat of Sir Robert Brisco, Bart. For obvious reasons I am only able to print the burden of this song.]

We'er aw fine fellows round Torkin,
   We're aw good fellows weel met ;
We're aw wet fellows round Torkin,
   Sae faikins we mun hev a sweat ;

Let's drink to the lasses about us,
   Till day's braid glare bids us start ;
We'll sup till the sallar be empty—
   Come, Dicky, lad, boddom the quart.

We're aw 'cute fellows round Torkin ;
   We're aw sharp fellows weel met ;
We're aw rare fellows round Torkin,
   Sae faikins we mun hev a sweat :

Let's drink to the lang, leame, and lazy,
   Deef, dum', black, brown, bleer-e'ed, and blin',
May they suin git weel weddet and beddet,
   If lads they can onic whoar fin'.

KING ROGER.

AIR : " Hallow Fair."

'Twas but tudder neet efter darknin',
    We sat owre a bleezin turf fire ;
Our deame she was stirrin' a cow-drink,
    Our Betty milk'd kye in the byre :
"Ay, fadder !" cried out our lal Roger,
    "I wish I was nobbet a king !"
"Wey, what wad t'e dui ?" says I, "Roger,
    Suppwose t'ou cud tek thy full swing ?"

"Furst, you sud be lword judge and bishop ;
    My mudder sud hev a gold crutch ;
I'd build for the peer fwok fine houses,
    And gie them—aye, iver sae much !
Our Betty sud wed Charley Miggins,
    And wear her stamp'd gown iv'ry day ;
Sec dancin we'd hev in the cockloft,
    Bill Adams the fiddle sud play.

"A posset I'd hev to my breakfast,
    And sup wid a breet siller spuin :
For dinner I'd hev a fat crowdy,
    And strang tea at mid efternuin :
I'd wear nice white cotton stockins,
    And new gambaleery clean shoes,
Wi' jimp lively black fustin britches,
    And iv'ry fine thing I cud choose.

" I'd hev mony thousands o' shippin',
    To sail the wide warl' aw about ;
I'd say to my soldiers, ' Gang owre seas,
    And kill the French dogs out and out !'
On our lang-tail'd naig I'd be mounted,
    My footmen in silver and green ;
And when I'd seen aw foreign countries,
    I'd mek Aggy Glaister my queen.

" Our meedow sud be a girt worchet,
    And grow nowte at aw but big plums ;
A schuil-house we'd build—as for maister,
    We'd e'en hing him up by the thums.
Joss Feddon sud be my head huntsman,
    We'd keep seben couple o' dogs,
And kill aw the hares i' the kingdom ;
    My mudder sud wear weel-greas'd clogs.

" Then Cursmas sud last, aye for iver !
    And Sundays we'd hae twice a week ;
The muin sud show leet aw the winter ;
    Our cat and our cwoley sud speak :
The peer fwok sud leeve widout workin,
    And feed on plum-puddin' and beef ;
Then aw wud be happy for sarten,
    There nowther cud be rwogue or thief."

Now thus run on little king Roger,
    But suin aw his happiness fled ;
A spark frae the fire brunt his knockle,
    And off he crap whingin' to bed :

Thus fares it wi' beath young and auld fwok,
  Frae king to the beggar we see ;
Just cross us i' th' midst o' our greatness,
  And peer wretched creatures are we !

THE PEET-SELLER'S LAMENT FOR
HIS MARE.

AIR : " Hey tutty tatty."

My bonny, bonny black meer's dead !
The thowt's e'en like to turn my head !
She led the peets, and gat me bread ;
          But what wull I dui now ?
And she was bworn when Jwohn was bworn,
Just nineteen years last Thursday mworn ;
Puir beast ! hed she got locks o' cworn,
          She'd been alive, I trow !

When young, just like a deil she ran ;
The car'-gear at Durdar she wan ;
That day saw me a happy man—
          Now tears gush frae my e'e :
For the meer's geane ; and my wife's geane ;
And Jwohn's a sodger far frae heame ;
Wi' brokken spirits !—left my leane !
          I've nin to comfort me !

When whyles I mounted on my yad,
I niver rode like yen stark mad;
We toddl'd on, and beath were glad
   To see our sonsie deame :
Our meer, the nebbors weel she knew;
And aw the dyke-backs whoar grass grew;
And when she'd pang'd her belly fou,
   How tow'rtly she cam heame!

Nae pamper'd beast e'er heeded we;
Nae wind or weet e'er dreeded she;
I niver cried " Wo-ah!" or "Jee!"
   She kent—aye, iv'ry turn.
And whyles I gat her teates o' hay,
And gev her watter twice-a-day :
But now she's dead! I'm wae to say;
   Then how can I but mourn?

Frae Tindal-fell twelve pecks she'd bring—
She was a yad fit for a king!
I niver struck her, silly thing!
   'Twas hard we twea sud part!
I's auld, and feal'd, and ragg'd, and peer;
I cannot raise anudder meer;
I cannot leeve anudder year,
   The loss 'ill break my heart!

ELIZABETH' BURTH-DAY.

AIR : " Lillibulero."

" Ay, Wulliam ! neist Monday's Elizabeth' burth-
day !
She is a nice lass, tho' she were nin o' mine.
We mun ax the Miss Dowson's, and auld Brodie'
young fwok :
I wish I'd but seav'd a swope geuseberry wine.
She'll be sebenteen ; what, she's got thro' her larnin ;
She dances as I did when first I kent thee.
As for Tom, her cruik'd billy, he stumps like a
cwoach-horse ;
We'll ne'er mek a man on him, aw we can dee."

" Hut, Jenny ! hod tongue o' thee ! praise nea sec
varment,
She won't men' a sark, but reads novels, proud
brat !
She dance ! what, she turns in her taes, thou peer
gonny,
Caw her Bet, 'twas the neame her auld granny
aye gat.
No, Tommy for my money ! he reads his Bible,
And hes sec a lovin'ly squint wid his een ;
He sheps as like me, as ae bean's like anudder ;
She snurls up her neb, just a shem to be seen !"

" Shaff, Wully ! that's fashion—t'ou kens nout about
　　it ;
She's streight as a resh, and as reed as a rwose,
She's sharp as a needle, and luiks like a leady ;
　　Thou talks, man—a lass cannot meake her awn
　　　　nwose !
She's delicate meade, and nit fit for the country ;
　　For Tom, he's knock-knee'd, wi' twea girt ass-
　　　　buird feet ;
God help them he sheps like ! they've little to brag
　　on ;
　　Tho' ours, I've oft thowt he was nit varra reet."

"O, Jen ! thou's run mad wi' thy gossips and
　　trumpery :
　　Our lal bit o' lan' we maun sell, I declare ;
I yence thowt thee an angel,—thou's turn'd just a
　　deevil,
　　Hes fash'd me reet lang, and oft vexes me sair :
This fashion and feastin' brings monie to ruin,
　　A duir o' my house they shall nit come within ;
As for Bet, if she dunnet gang off till a sarvice,
　　When I's dead and geane she shall nit hev a pin."

"Stop, Wull ! whea was't brong thee that fortune ?
　　peer gomas !
　　Just thirteen gud yacres as lig to the sun ;
When I tuik up wi' thee, I'd lost peer Gwordy Glossip,
　　I've rued sin' that hour to the kurk when we run :

Were thou cauld and coffin'd, I'd suin git a better ;
Sae creep off to bed, nit a word let us hear !
They shall come, if God spare us, far mair than I
   mention'd—
Elizabeth' burth-day but comes yence a-year."

———

BORROWDALE JWOHNY.

AIR : "I am a young fellow."

I's Borrowdale Jwohny, just cumt up to Lunnon,
   Nay, girn nit at me, for fear I laugh at you ;
I've seen knaves donn'd i' silks, and gud men gang
   in tatters,
   The truth we sud tell, and gie auld Nick his due.
Nan Watt pruiv'd wi' bairn—what, they caw'd me
   the fadder ;
   Thinks I, *shekum filthy !* be off in a tryce !
Nine Carel bank nwotes mudder slipt i' my pocket,
   And fadder neist gev me reet holesome advice.

Says he, " keep frae t' lasses ! and ne'er luik ahint
   thee."
" We're deep as the best o' them, fadder," says I.
They pack'd up ae sark, Sunday weastcwoat, twea
   neckcloths,
   Wot bannock, cauld dumplin', and top stannin'
   pie :

I mounted black filly, bade God bless the auld fwok,
    Cries fadder, " T'ou's larn'd, Jwohn, and hes
        nowte to fear ;
Caw and see cousin Jacop ! he's got aw the money ;
    He'll git thee sum guverment pleace, to be seer !"

I stopp'd on the fell, tuik a lang luik at Skiddaw,
    And neist at the schuil-house amang the esh trees ;
Last thing saw the smuik rising up frae our chimley,
    And fun' aw quite queer, wi' a heart ill at ease :
But summet within me cried, Pou up thy spirits !
    There's luck, says auld Lizzy, in feacin' the sun ;
Tou's young, lish, and cliver, may wed a fine leady,
    And come heame a Nabob—aye, sure as a gun !

Knowin' manners, what, I doff'd my hat to aw
    strangers,
    Wid a spur on my heel, a yek siplin in han',
It tuik me nine days and six hours comin' up-bank,
    At the *Whorns*—aye, 'twas *Highget*, a chap bad
        me stan' :
Says he, " How's all friends in the North, honest
    Johnny ? '
    Odswunters ! I says, what, ye divent ken me !
I paid twea white shillin's, and fain was to see him,
    Nit thinkin on't rwoad onie 'quaintance to see.

Neist thing, what big kurks, gilded cwoaches, hee
    houses,
  And fwok runnin' thro' other, like Carel fair ;
I ax'd a smart chap⁻whoar to find cousin Jacep,
    Says he, " Clown, go look !" " Friend," says I,
    " tell me where ?"
Fadder' letter to Jacep hed got nae *subscription*,
  Sae, when I was glowrin' and siz'lin about,
A white-feac'd young lass, aw dress'd out like a
    leady,
    Cried, " Pray, Sir, step in !" but I wish I'd kept
    out.

She pou'd at a bell, like our kurk-bell it sounded,
    In com a sarvant lass and she worder'd some
    wine ;
Says I, I's nit dry, sae, pray Madam, excuse me ;
  Nay, what she insisted I sud stop and dine.
She meade varra free—'twas a shem and a byzen !
  I thowt her in luive wi' my *parson*, for sure ;
And promis'd to caw agean ;—as for black filly,
  (Wad onie believ't) she was stown frae the duir !

Od dang't ! waur than that—when I greap'd my
    breek pocket,
  I fan fadder' watch, and the nwotes were aw gean ;
It was neet, and I luik'd lang and sair for kent
    feaces,
  But Borrowdale fwok I cud niver see neane.

I slept on the flags, just ahint the kurk-corner,
  A chap wid a girt stick and lantern com by,
He caw'd me peace-breaker—says I tou's a lear—
  In a pleace like a cellar they fworc'd me to lie.

Nae caff bed or blanket for silly pilgarlic;
  Deil a wink cud I sleep, nay, nor yet see a stime :
Neist day I was ta'en to the Narration Offish,
  When a man in a wig said, I'd duin a sad crime.
Then ane ax'd my neame, and he put on his speckets,
  Says I, "Jwohny Cruckdyke—I's Borrowdale
    bworn ;"
Whea think ye it prov'd but me awn cousin Jacep,
  He seav'd me frae t' gallows, ay that varra mworn.

He spak to my lword, some hard words quite
    outlandish,
  Then caw'd for his cwoach, and away we ruid
    heame ;
He ax'd varra kind efter fadder and mudder,
  I said they were bravely, and neist saw his deame ;
She's aw puff and powder ; as for cousin Jacep,
  He's got owre much gear to teake nwotish o' me ;
But if onie amang ye sud want a lish sarvant,
  Just bid me a weage—I'll uphod ye, we's 'gree.

January, 1807.

SOLDIER YEDDY.

Air : "The widow can bake."

Peer Yeddy was browte up a fadderless bairn,
His jacket blue duffle, his stockin's cworse gairn ;
His mudder, sad greaceless ! liv'd near Talkin Tarn,
    But ne'er did a turn for her Yeddy.

Weel shep'd, and fair feac'd, wid a bonny blue e'e,
Honest-hearted, aye merry, still tidy was he ;
But nae larnin' had gotten, nor kent A B C ;
    There's owre monie like silly Yeddy.

Suin tir'd o' the cwoal-pit, and drivin' a car',
Won by feathers, cockades, and the fuil'ries o' war,
He wad see fine fwok, and grand pleaces afar—
    The bad warl' was aw new to lal Yeddy.

How temptin' the liquor, and bonny bank nwote !
How temptin' the powder, sash, gun, and reed cwoat !
Then the Frenchmen, die bin them, we'll kill the
    whole twote !
    These, these were his thowts, honest Yeddy.

Awhile wi' his cronies he'll smuik, laugh, and sing,
Tell of wonders, and brag of his country and king,
And swagger, and larn of new oaths a sad string—
    These little avail simple Yeddy.

For suin he may sing to anudder guess-tune,
His billet a bad yen, his kelter aw duin;
And faint at his post by the pale winter muin,
    Nae comfort awaits luckless Yeddy.

When time steals his colour, and meks his pow grey,
May he tell merry stories, nor yence rue the day,
When he wander'd, peer lad! frae the fell side away;
    This, this is my wish for young Yeddy.

Of lads sec as him may we ne'er be in want,
And a brave soldier's pocket of brass ne'er be scant;
Nit the brags o' proud Frenchmen auld England
    can daunt,
    While we've plenty like young soldier Yeddy.

THE LAST NEW SHOON OUR BETTY GAT.

AIR: "Tak your auld cloak about ye."

The last new shoon our Betty gat,
    They pinch her feet, the deil may care!
What, she mud hae them leady like,
    'Tho' she hes cworns for ivermair!
Nae black gairn stockins will she wear,
    They maun be white, and cotton fine!
This meks me think o' other times,
    The happy days o' auld lang syne!

Our dowter, tui, a palace* bowte,
  A gud reed cloak she cannot wear ;
And stays, she says, spoil leady's sheps—
  Oh ! it wad mek a parson swear.
Nit ae han's turn o' wark she'll dui,
  She'll nowther milk nor sarra t' swine—
The country's puzzen'd round wi' pride !
  For lasses work'd reet hard lang syne !

We've three gud rooms in our clay house,
  Just big eneugh for sec as we ;
They'd hev a parlour built wi' bricks,
  I mud submit—what cud I dee ?
The sattle neist was thrown aside,
  It meeght hae sarra'd me and mine ;
My mudder thowt it mens'd a house—
  But we think shem o' auld lang syne !

We us'd to gae to bed at dark,
  And ruse agean at four or five ;
The mworn's the only time for wark,
  If fwok are hilthy and wad thrive :
Now we get up—nay, God kens when !
  And nuin's owre suin for us to dine ;
I's hungry or the pot's hawf boil'd,
  And wish for times like auld lang syne.

Deuce tek the fuil-invented tea !
  For twice a-day we that mun have :
Then taxes get sae monstrous hee,
  The deil a plack yen now can seave !
      * Pelisse.

There's been nae luck throughout the lan',
Sin' fwok mun like their betters shine ;
French fashions mek us parfet fuils ;
We're caff and san' to auld lang syne.

THE BUCK O' KINGWATTER.

[AIR: "The Breckans of Brampton."--The vale of King-
water lies near Gilsland, in the immediate neighbourhood of
Triermaine Tower and Askerton Castle. "The lordly halls
of Triermaine" supplied the title to one of Sir Walter Scott's
poems.]

When I was single, I rid a fine nag,
And was caw'd the Buck o' Kingwatter ;
Now the cwoat o' my back hes got but ae sleeve,
And my breeks are aw in a tatter.
Sing, Oh! the lasses! the lazy lasses!
Keep frae the lasses o' Bran'ton :
I ne'er wad hae married, that day I married,
But I was young, fuilish, and wanton.

I courted a lass—an angel I thowt—
She's turn'd out the picture of evil ;
She geapes, yen may count iv'ry tuith in her head,
And shouts fit to freeten the deevil.
Sing, Oh, the lasses, &c.

To-day she slipt out, some 'bacco to buy,
  And bade me mind rock the cradle ;
I cowp'd owre asleep, but suin she com in,
  And brak aw my head wi' the ladle.
          Sing, Oh, the lasses, &c.

I ne'er hed a heart to hannel a gun,
  Or I'd run away and leave her.
She pretends to win purns, but that's aw fun,
  They say she's owre kind wi' the weaver.
          Sing, Oh, the lasses, &c.

I dinnerless gang ae hawf o' the week ;
  If we git a bit meat on a Sunday,
She cuts me nae mair than wad physic a snipe ;
  Then we've 'tatey and point iv'ry Monday.
          Sing, Oh, the lasses, &c.

Tho' weary o' life, wi' this gud-for-nowte wife,
  I wish I cud git sec anudder ;
And then I cud gie the deevil the teane,
  For takin' away the tudder !
          Sing, Oh, the lasses, &c.

MADAM JANE.

AIR: "I will hae a wife."

Money meks us bonny,
    Money meks us glad;
Be she auld or ugly,
    Money brings a lad.
When I'd ne'er a penny,
    Deil a lad hed I—
Pointin' aye at Jenny,
    Laughin' they flew by.

Money causes flatt'ry,
    Money meks us vain;
Money changes aw things—
    Now I'm *Madam Jane.*
Sen auld Robby left me
    Houses, fields, nit few,
Lads thrang round i' clusters,
    I'm a beauty now!

Money meks us merry,
    Money meks us bra';
Money gits us sweethearts—
    That's the best of a'!
I hae fat and slender,
    I hae shwort and tall;
I hae rake and miser—
    I despise them all!

Money they're aw seeking,
  Money they's git neane ;
Money sends them sneaking
  Efter *Madam Jane!*
There's ane puir and bashfu',
  I hae i' my e'e ;
He's git han' and siller,
  Gin he fancies me.

YOUNG SUSY.

AIR : "Daintie Davie."

Young Susy is a bonny lass,
A canny lass, a tidy lass,
A mettl'd lass, a hearty lass,
  As ony yen can see ;
A clean-heel'd lass, a weel-spok lass,
A buik-larn'd lass, a kurk-gawn lass,
I watna how it com to pass,
  She's meade a fuil o' me.
  I's tir'd o' workin', ploughin', sowin',
  Deetin', dykin', threshin', mowin' ;
  Seeghin', greanin', niver knowin'
    What I's gawn to de.

I met her—aye, 'twas this day week !
Od die ! thowt I, I'll try to speak ;
But tried in vain the teale to seek,
      For sec a lass is she !
Her jet black hair hawf hides her brow,
Her een just thirl yen thro' and thro'—
But oh ! her cheeks and cherry mou'
      Are far owre sweet to see !
            I's tir'd o' workin', &c.

Oh, cud I put her in a sang !
To hear her praise the heale day lang,
She mud consent to kurk to gang ;
      Their's puirer fwok than me !
But I can nowther rhyme nor rave,
Luive meks yen sec a coward slave ;
I'd better far sleep i' my grave—
      But, oh, that munnet be !
   I's tir'd o' workin', plowin', sowin',
   Deetin', dykin, threshin', mowin' ;
   Seeghin', greanin', niver knowin'
      What I's gawn to de.

PEGGY PEN.

AIR : "Miss Forbes' Farewell."

The muin shone breet the tudder neet ;
   The kye was milk't, aw t' wark was duin ;
I wesh'd my feace, an' cwom't my hair,
   Threw off my clogs, put on greas'd shoon ;
The clock struck eight, as out I stule ;
   The rwoad I tuik, reet weel I ken ;
An' cros't the watter, clam the hill,
   I' whops to meet wi' Peggy Pen.

When i' the wood, I hard some talk ;
   They cutter'd on, but varra low ;
I hid mysel' ahint a yek,
   An' Peggy wi' a chap suin saw :
He smackt her lips, she cried, " Give owre !
   We lasses aw are pleagut wi' men ;"
I tremlin' stuid, but dursen't speak,
   Tho' fain wad coddled Peggy Pen !

He cawt her Marget, sometimes Miss ;
   He spak quite fine, and kiss'd her han' ;
He bragg'd of aw his fadder hed ;
   I sigh'd ; for we've nae house or lan' :
Said he, " My dear, I've watch'd you oft,
   And seen you link through wood and glen,
With one George Moor, a rustic poor,
   Not fit to wait on sweet Miss Pen !"

She drew her han', and turn'd her roun' ;
   " Let's hae nae mair sec talk," says she ;
" Tho' Gwordie Muir be nobbet puir,
   He's dearer nor a prince to me !   .
My fadder scauls, mworn, nuin, an' neet ;
   My mudder fratches sair—what then ?
This warl's gear cud niver buy
   Frae Gworge, the luive o' Peggy Pen !"

" O Miss ! " says he, " forget such fools ;
   Nor heed the awkward, stupid clown ;
If such a creetcher spoke to me,
   I'd quickly knock the booby down."
" Come on," says I, " thy strength e'en try ;
   An' head owre heels sec chaps I'd sen' :
Lug off thy cwoat : I'll feight aw neet,
   Wi' three, like thee, for Peggy Pen."

Now off he flew ; my arms I threw
   Around her waist ; away we went ;
I ax'd her, if she durst be mine ;
   She squeez'd my han', an' gev consent :
We tawkt and jwokt, as lovers sud :
   We parted at their awn byre en' ;
And ere anudder month be owre,
   She'll change, to Muir, frae Peggy Pen !

THREESCORE AND NINETEEN.

AIR by the Author.

Aye, aye, I's feeble grown,
   And feckless—weel I may !
I's threescwore and nineteen,
   Aye, just this varra day !
I hae nae teeth, my meat to chew,
   But little sarras me :
The best thing I eat or drink,
   Is just a cup o' tea !

Aye, aye, the bairns mak gam,
   And pleague me suin and late ;
Men fwok I like i' my heart,
   But bairns and lasses hate !
This gown o' mine's lang i' the waist,
   Auld-fashion'd i' the sleeve ;
It meks me luik like fourscwore,
   I varily believe !

Aye, aye, what I's deef,
   My hearin's quite geane ;
I's fash'd wi' that sad cough aw neet,
   But little I complain.
I smuik a bit, and cough a bit,
   And then I try to spin ;
And then I daddle to the duir,
   And then I daddle in.

Aye, aye, I wonder much,
   How women can git men ;
I've tried for threescwore years and mair,
   But niver cud git yen.
Deil tek the cat—what is she at ?
   Lie quiet on the chair :
I thowt it e'en was Daniel Strang,
   Comin' up the stair' !

Aye, aye, I've bed and box,
   And kist, and clock, and wheel,
And tub, and rock, and stuil, and pan,
   And chair, and dish, and reel ;
And luiking-glass, and cham'er pot,
   And bottles for smaw beer ;
Mouse trap, saut box, kettle, and—
   That's Danny sure I hear !

Aye, aye, he's young enough,
   But, oh, a reet nice man ;
And I wad ne'er be cauld in bed,
   Cud I but marry Dan !
Deuce tek that cough, that weary cough!
   It niver lets me be ;
I's kilt wi' that and gravel beath—
   Oh, Daniel, come to me !

CAREL FAIR.

AIR : "Woo'd and married and a'."

My neame's Jurry Jurden, frae Threlket ;
Just swat down, and lissen my sang ;
I'll mappen affword some divarsion,
And tell ye how monie things gang.

Crops o' aw maks are gud ; tateys lang as lapstens. and dry as meal. Times are sae sae ; for the thin-chop'd, hawf-neak'd trimlin' beggars flock to our house, like bees to t' hive : and our Cwoley bit sae monie, I just tuck'd him i' th' worchet. Mudder boils t'em a knop o' Lunnen Duns, ivery day ; and fadder gies t'em t' barn to lig in. If onie be yebel to work, wey he pays t'em reet weel. Fwok sud aw dui as they'd be duin tui ; an' it's naturable to beg, rayder nor starve or steal ; efter aw the rattle !

Some threep et the times 'll git better ;
And laugh to see onie repine ;
I's nae pollytishin, that's sarten,
But England seems in a decline !

I ruise afwore three, tudder mwornin',
And went owre to see Carel Fair ;
I'd heard mony teales o' thur dandies—
Odswinge ! how they mek the fwok stare !

Thur flay-crows wear lasses' stays : and buy my Lword Wellinten's buits ; cokert, but nit snout-bandet. My sartey ! sec a laugh I gat, to see a tarrier meakin' watter on yen o' the'r legs ! They're seerly mongrels, hawf-monkey breed : shep't for awt' warl' like wasps, smaw i' t' middle. To see them paut pauten about, puts me i' min' o' our aul' gander ; and if they meet a bonny lass, they darn't turn roun' to luik at her. The "Turk's Heed" and "Tir'd Spwortsman" are bonny signs, but a dandy wad be far mair comical ; efter aw the rattle !

But, shaff o' sec odd trinkum-trankums!
Thur hawf-witted varmen bang aw;
They'd freeten aul' Nick, sud t'ey meet him—
A dandy's just fit for a show!

I neist tuik a glowre 'mang the butchers,
An' glym'd at the'r lumps o' fat meat;
They've aw maks the gully can dive at—
It meks peer fwok hungry to see 't.

"What d'ye buy! what d'ye buy?"—"Weya, butcher,
wul t'e be out at our en' o' t' country, suin! we've a faymish
bull, nobbet eleben year aul'; twea braid-back't tips, an' a
bonny sew." "Nae bull, tips, or swine for me!"—"Hes t'e
got any coves' heeds to sell, butcher?" "Wey nay, Tommy;
but t'ou hes yen atop o' thy shou'ders! What d'ye buy? what
d'ye buy? here's beef fit for a bishop; mutton for a markiss;
lam' for a lword; aw sworts for aw maks; hee an' low, yen
an' aw: nobbet sebenpence a pun': efter aw the rattle!"

While peer fwok was starin' about t'em,
Up hobbles an aul' chap, an' begs—
Oh! wad our girt heeds o' the nayshen
Just set the peer fwok on their legs.

An odd seet I saw, 'twas t' naig market,
Whoar aw wer' as busy as bees;
Sec lurryan, an' trottin', an' scamp'rin'—
Lord help t'em!—they're meade up o' lees!

"Try a canter, Deavie."—"Whoar gat t'e t' powny, Tim?
—"Wey at Stegshe."—"That's a blud meer," says aul'
Breakshe, "she was gitten by Shrimp, an' out o' Madam
Wagtail; she wan t' King's Plate at Donkister, tudder year."
—"Wan the deevil!" says yen tull him, "T'ou means
t' bridle at Kingmuir, min!"—"Here's a nag! nobbet just
nwotish his een! he can see through a nine inch waw. Fuils

tell o' fortifications ; what he hes a breest like a fiftification. Dud ye iver see yen cock sec a tail, widout a peppercworn ?" "What dus t'e ax for 'em, canny man ?"—"Wey, he 's weel worth twonty pun' ; but I'll teake hawf."—"Twonty deevils ! I'll gi'e thec twonty shillin' ; efter aw the rattle !"

What aw trades are bad as horse-cowpers ;
  They mek the best bargain they can ;
Fwok say, it's the seame in aw countries—
  Man likes to draw kelter frae man !

Neist daunderin' down to the Cow Fair,
  A famish rough rumpus I saw ;
For Rickergeate lwoses her charter,
  Sud theer be nae feightin' at aw.

Aa ! what a hay-bay ! 'twas just like the battle o' Watter-lew. Men an' women, young an' aul', ran frae aw quarters. Theer was sec shoutin', thrustin', pushin', an' squeezin' ; what they knock'd down staws ; an' brak shop windows aw to flinders. Thur leed-heedit whups dui muckle mischief : a sairy beggar gat a bloody nwose an' brokken teeth i' the fray. Hilltop Tom, and Low-gill Dick, the twea feightin' rap-scallions, wer' lugget off by the bealies, to my lword Mayor's offish ; an' thrussen into the black whol. I whop they'll lig theer : for it's weel nae lives wer' lost ; efter aw the rattle !

Shem o' them ! thur peer country hanniels,
  That slink into Carel to feight !
De'il bin them ! when free frae hard labour,
  True plishure sud be their delyte.

Theer was geapin' an' stairin', 'mang aw maks—
  "Aa ! gies t'y fist, Ellek ! how's t'ou !"
"Wey, aw bais'd, an' bluitert, an' queerish ;
  "We'll tek a drop gud mountain dew."

"Sees t'e, Ellek, theer's t' peer luikin' chap, et meks aw t'
bits o' Cummerlan' ballets!"—"The deevil! fye, Jobby,
let's off frev him, for fear!"— "Here's yer whillimer! lank
an' lean, but cheap an' clean!" says yen. "Buy a pair of
elegant shun, young gentleman," cries a dandy snob, "they
wer' meade for Mr. Justice Grunt. Weages are hee, an'
ledder's dear; but they're nobbet twelve shillin'." Then a
fat chap wid a hammer, selt clocks, cubberts, teables, chairs,
pots and pans for nowte at aw. What, I seed fadder talkin'
to t' lawyer, an' gowl'd till my e'en was sair: but nae ill was
duin; efter aw the rattle!

Then peer bits o' hawf-brokken farmers
    In leggin's, wer' struttin' about;
Wer' times gud, they'd aw become dandies—
    We'll ne'er leeve to see that, I doubt!

Sec screapin', and squeekin', 'mang t' fiddlers;
    I crap up the stairs, to be seer;
But suin trottet down by the waiter,
    For de'il a bit caprin' was theer.

What lads and lasses are far owre proud to dance, now-a-
days. I stowtert ahint yen dess't out like a gingerbreed
queen, an' when I gat a gliff at her, whea sud it be but Jenny
Muirthet, my aul' sweetheart. I tried to give her a buss, but
cuddent touch her muzzle; for she wore yen o' thur meal
scowp bonnets. She ax'd me to buy her a parryswol; sae we
off to the dandy shop, an' I gat her yen, forby a ridiculous.
Jenny'll hev a mountain o' money; an', my stars, she's a
walloper! Aa! just like a house en'! As for me, I's nobbet
a peer lillyprushen; but she'll be mine, efter aw the rattle!

Sae we link'd, an' we laugh'd, an' we chatter'd;
    Few hussies, like Jenny, ye'll see;
O hed we but taen off to Gretna,
    Nin wad been sae happy as we!

We went thro' the big kurk an' cassel ;
And neist tuik a rammel thro' t' streets :
What, Carel's the pleace for fine houses,
But monie a peer body yen meets.

Ay ! yen in tatters, wi' ae e'e, shoutet, "Here's last speech,
confession, and deein' words o' Martha Mumps : she was
hang't for committin' a reape on—Hut, shaff ! I forgit his
neame." Anudder tatterdemalion says, "Come buy a full
chinse Indy muslin ; nobbet sixpence hawfpenny a yard !"
Jenny bowt yen, an' it was rotten as muck. Then theer was
bits o' things wi' their neddys, and rwoarin' up t' lanes,
"Bleng-ki-ship cwoals !" And chaps cawin' "Watter !
watter !" it mun be that meks't yell sae smaw. Then they'll
sell puzzen for gin ; what it hes see a grip o' the gob, it's like
to mek fwok shek their heeds off. They hannel brass an'
uwotes, but ther's nee siller i' Carel. See cheatin', stealin',
wheedlin', leein', rwoarin', swearin', drinkin', feightin', meks
Fairs nowt et dow ; efter aw the rattle !

Thro' life we hev aw maks amang us ;
Sad changes ilk body mun share :
To-day we're just puzzen'd wi' plishure !
To-mworn we're bent double wi' care !

September, 1819.

THE DAWTIE.

Air : "I'm o'er young to marry yet."

"Tho' weel I like ye, Jwohny lad,
I cannot, munnet marry yet !
My peer auld mudder's unco bad,
Sae we a while mun tarry yet ;

For ease or comfort she has neane—
Life's just a lang, lang neet o' pain ;
I munnet leave her aw her leane,
   And wunnet, wunnet marry yet !"

"O Jenny ! dunnet break this heart,
   And say, we munnet marry yet ;
Thou cannot act a jillet's part—
   Why sud we tarry, tarry yet !
Think, lass, of aw the pains I feel ;
I've lik'd thee lang, nin kens how weel !
For thee, I'd feace the varra deil—
   O say not, we mun tarry yet !"

"A weddet life's oft dearly bowte ;
   I cannot, munnet marry yet ;
Ye hae but little—I hae nowte,
   Sae, we a while mun tarry yet !
My heart's yer awn, ye needn't fear,
But let us wait anudder year,
And luive, and toil, and screape up gear—
   We munnet, munnet marry yet !

"'Twas but yestreen, my mudder said,
   'O, dawtie ! dunnet marry yet !
I'll suin lig i' my last cauld bed ;
   Tou's aw my comfort—tarry yet !'
Whene'er I steal out o' her seet,
She seeghs, and sobs, and nowte gangs reet—
Whisht !—that's her feeble voice ;—gud neet ;
   We munnet, munnet marry yet !"

THE CODBECK WEDDIN'.

[AIR : " Andrew Carr."—The bridegroom, " weaver Joe
Bewley," died in the neighbourhood of Caldbeck about 1870,
having reached his ninetieth year. However "white" or
pale-faced Joe might be when the parson buckled him to
Dalton's "lish dowter," he could always show plenty of
metal in after life, when occasion required it. He was pas-
sionately fond of fox-hunting, and used to boast that he
hunted with John Peel, on Scratchmere Scar, when the
veritable fox was killed which is celebrated in Woodcock
Grave's song. A short time before his death, on being told
that the Cumberland foxhounds had passed close to his house
only a few hours before, he cried again for vexation that he
had missed the opportunity of "hevin' anudder gud run efter
t' hoonds !"]

They sing of a weddin' at Worton,
  Whoar aw was feight, fratchin', and fun ;
Feegh ! sec a yen we've hed at Codbeck ;
  As niver was under the sun :
The bridegruim was weaver Joe Bewley,
  He com frae about Lowthet Green ;
The bride, Jwohny Dalton' lish dowter,
  And Betty was weel to be seen.

Sec patchin', and weshin', and bleachin',
  And starchin', and darnin' auld duds ;
Some lasses thowt lang to the weddin'—
  Unax'd, others sat i' the suds.
There were tweescore and seben invited,
  God speed t'em, 'gainst Cursenmass-day ;
Dobson' lads, tui, what they mun com hidder—
  I think they were better away.

Furst thing Oggle Willy, the fiddler,
  Caw'd in, wi' auld Jonathan Strang;
Neist stiff and stout, lang, leame, and lazy,
  Frae aw parts com in wi' a bang;—
Frae Brocklebank, Faulders, and Newlands,
  Frae Hesket, Burkheads, and the Height,
Frae Warnell, Stairnmire, Nether Welton,
  And aw't way frae Eytonfield-street.*

Furst auld Jwohny Dawton we'll nwotish,
  And Mary, his canny douse deame;
Son Wully, and Mally, his sister;
  Goffet' wife, muckle Nanny by neame;
Wully Sinclair, Smith Lytle, Jwohn Aitchin,
  Tom Ridley, Joe Sim, Peter Weir,
Gworge Goffet, Jwohn Bell, Miller Dyer,
  Joe Head and Ned Bulman were there.

We'd hay-cruiks, and hentails, and hanniels,
  And nattlers that fuddle for nowte;
Wi' skeapgreaces, skybels, and scruffins,
  Wi' maffs better fed far than taught;
We'd lads that wad eat for a weager,
  Or feight, ay, till blood to the knees;
Fell-siders, and Sowerby riff-raff,
  That de'il a bum-bealie dare seize.

The bride hung her head, and luik'd sheepish,
  The bridegruim as white as a clout;
The bairns aw glym'd thro' the kurk windows,
  The parson was varra devout:

* Names of Cumberland villages.

The ring was lost out of her pocket,
　The bride meade a bonny te-dee ;
Cries Goffet' wife, " Mine's meade o' pinchbeck,
　And, la ye ; it fits till a tee."

Now buckl'd, wi' fiddlers afwore them,
　They gev Michael Crosby a caw ;
Up spak canny Bewley, the bridegruim,
　" Git slocken'd, lad, fadder pays aw."
We drank till aw seem'd blue about us,
　We're aw merry devils, tho' peer ;
Michael's wife says, " Widout onie leein',
　A duck mud ha'e swam on the fleer."

Now, aw bacco'd owre, and hawf-drucken,
　The men fwok wad needs kiss the bride ;
Joe Head, that's aye rackon'd best spokesman,
　Whop'd " gud wad the couple betide."
Says Michael, " I's reet glad to see you,
　Suppwosin' I gat ne'er a plack."
Cries t' wife, " That 'll nowther pay t' brewer,
　Nor git bits o' sarks to yen's back."

The bride wad dance *Coddle me Cuddie.*
　A threesome then caper'd Scotch reels ;
Peter Weir cleek'd up auld Mary Dalton,
　Like a cock round a hen neist he steals ;
Jwohn Bell yelp'd out 'Sowerby Lassies ;'
　Young Jwosep a lang country dance,
He'd got his new pumps Smithson meade him ;
　And fain wad show how he cud prance.

To march round the town, and keep swober,
    The woman fwok thowt was but reet;
" Be wise, dui, for yence," says Jwohn Dyer,
    The bridegruim mud ride shou'der heet ;—
The younger-mak lurried ahint them,
    Till efter them Bell meade a brek ;
Tom Ridley was aw baiz'd wi' drinkin',
    And plung'd off the steps i' the beck.

To Hudless's now off they sizell'd,
    And there gat far mair than eneugh ;
Miller Hodgson suin brunt the punch ladle,
    And full'd iv'ry glass wid his leuf ;
He thowt he was teakin' his mouter,
    And de'il a bit conscience hes he ;
They prim'd him wi' stiff punch and jollop,
    Till Sally Scott thowt he wad dee.

Joe Sim rwoar'd out, " Bin, we've duin wonders !
    Our Mally's turn'd howe i' the weame."
Wi' three strings atween them, the fiddlers
    Strack up, and they reel'd towerts heame ;
Miner Lytle wad now hoist a standert—
    Peer man ! he cud nit daddle far,
But stuck in a pant 'buin the middle,
    And yen tuik him heame in a car.

For dinner we'd stew'd geuse and haggish,
    Cow'd-leady, and het bacon pie,
Boil'd fluiks, tatey-hash, beastin' puddin',
    Saut salmon, and cabbish ; forbye

Pork, pancakes, black puddin's, sheep trotters,
  And custert, and mustert, and veal,
Grey-pez keale, and lang apple dumplin's—
  I wish ivery yen far'd as weel.

The bride geavin' aw round about her,
  Cries, " Wuns ! we forgat butter sops !"
The bridegruim fan' nae time for talkin',
  But wi' stannin' pie greas'd his chops.
We'd lopper'd milk, skimm'd milk, and kurn'd milk,
  Well-watter, smaw beer, aw at yence ;
"Shaff ! bring yell in piggens," rwoars Dalton,
  De'il tak them e'er cares for expense."

Now aw cut and cleek'd frae their neybors,
  'Twas even down thump, pull and haul ;
Joe Head gat a geuse aw togidder,
  And off he crap into the faul ;"
Muckle Nanny cried, "Shem o' sec weastry !"
  The ladle she brak owre ill Bell ;
Tom Dalton sat thrang in a corner,
  And eat nar the weight of his-sel' !

A hillibuloo was now started,
  'Twas, " Rannigal ! whea cares for tee ?"
" Stop, Tommy—whea's wife was i' th' carras ?
  T'ou'd ne'er been a man but for me !"
" Od dang thee !"—" To jail I cud send thee !
  Peer Scraffles !"—" Thy lan' grows nae gurse !"
" Ne'er ak ! it's my awn, and it's paid for !
  But whea was't stuil auld Tim Jwohn' purse !"

Ned Bulman wad feight wi' Gworge Goffet—
  Peer Gwordy he nobbet stript thin,
And luik'd like a cock out o' fedder,
  But suin gat a weel-bleaken'd skin ;
Neist Sanderson fratch'd wi' a hay-stack,
  And Deavison fuight wi' the whins ;
Smith Lytle fell out wi' the cobbles,
  And peel'd aw the bark off his shins.

The hay-bay was now somewhat sided,
  And young fwok the music men miss'd,
They'd drucken like fiddlers in common,
  And fawn owre ayont an aul' kist ;
Some mair fwok that neet was a-missin',
  Than Wully, and Jonathan Strang—
But decency whispers, " What matter !
  T'ou munnet put them in thy sang."

Auld Dalton thowt he was at Carel,
  Says he, " Jacob, see what's to pay ;
Come, wosler ! heaste—git out the horses,
  We'll e'en tek the rwoad, and away."
He cowp'd off his stuil like a san' bag,
  Tom Ridley beel'd out, " De'il may care !"
For a whart o' het yell, and a stick in't,
  Dick Simson 'll tell ye far mair.

Come, bumper the Cummerlan' lasses,
  Their marrows can seldom be seen ;
And he that won't feight to defend them,
  I wish he may ne'er want black e'en.

May our murry-neets, clay-daubins, reaces,
  And weddin's, aye finish wi' glee ;
And when owte's amang us worth nwotish,
  Lang may I be present to see.

THE ILL-GIEN WIFE.

AIR : "My wife has ta'en the gee."

A toilsome life for thirty years,
  I patiently hev spent,
As onie yen o' onie rank,
  I' this wide warl' e'er kent ;
For when at heame, or when away,
  Nae peace there is for me ;
I's pester'd wi' an *ill-gien wife*,
  That niver lets me be :
    Aye teazin', ne'er ceasin',
      Like an angry sea ;
Nae kurk-bell e'er hed sec a tongue ;
  And oft it deafens me !

      .   .   .

When young, I wish'd for wife and weans,
  But now the thowt I scworn ;
Thank Heav'n, a bairn o' owther sex
  To me she ne'er hes bworn !

Like fuils we wish our youth away,
  When happy we mud be—
Aw ye that's pleagu'd wi' scauldin wives,
  I wish ye suin set free !
Grin, grinnin' !—din, dinnin' !
  Toil and misery !
Better feed the kurk-yard worms
  Than leeve sec slaves as we !

I's past aw wark, it's hard to want,
  And auld and peer am I ;
But happiness i' this vile warl,
  Nae gear cud iver buy :
O were I on some owre-sea land,
  Nae woman near to see,
At pride an' grandeur I wad smile,
  An' thanks to Heav'n wad gie :
O woman ! foe to man !
  A blessin' thou sud be ;
But wae to him that wears thy chain,
  Peer wretch unblest like me !

When wintry blasts blow loud an' keen,
  I's fain to slink frae heame ;
An' rayder feace the angry storm,
  Than her I hate to neame :
While she wi' sland'rous cronies met,
  Sits hatchin' monie a lee ;
The seet wad flay auld Nick away,
  Or vex a saint to see.

Puff, puffin'!—snuff, snuffin'!
    Ne'er frae mischief free;
How weak is lwordly boastin' man,
    On sec to cast an e'e!

If to a neybor's house I steal,
    To crack a while at neet,
She hurries to me like a deil,
    An' flays the fwok to see't;
Whate'er I dui, whate'er I say,
    Wi' her a faut mun be;
I freet an' freet baith neet an' day,
    But seldom clwose an e'e:
Wake, wakin'!—shake, shakin'!
    Then she teks the gee;
He's happy that live's aw his leane,
    Compar'd wi' chaps like me.

To stop the never-ceasin' storm,
    I brong her cousin here;
She aw but brak the wee thing's heart,
    An' cost her monie a tear:
If chance a frien' pops in his head,
    Off to the duir she'll flee;
She snarls like onie angry cat,
    An' sair I's vex'd to see!
Now fratchin', neist scratchin',
    Oft wi' bleaken'd e'e;
I pray auld Nick hed sec a deame,
    I trow he vex'd wad be!

How blithe man meets the keenest ills,
  In this shwort voyage o' life,
And thinks nae palace like his heame,
  Blest wid a kindly wife :
But sure the greatest curse hard fate
  To onie man can gie,
Is sec a filthy slut as mine,
  That ne'er yence comforts me ;
Lads jeerin', lasses sneerin',
  Cuckold some caw me ;
I scrat an auld grey achin' pow,
  But darn't say they lee.

They're happy that hev tidy wives,
  To keep peer bodies clean ;
But mine's a freetfu' lump o' filth,
  Her marrow ne'er was seen :
Ilk dud she wears upon her back,
  Is poison to the e'e ;
Her smock's like auld Nick's nuttin' bag,
  The deil a word I lee :
Dour an' dirty—house aw clarty !
  See her set at tea,
Her feace defies beath seape and san',
  To mek't just fit to see !

A bite o' meat I munnet eat,
  Seave what I cuik mysel ;
Ae patch or clout she'll nit stick on,
  Sae heame's just like a hell :

By day or neet, if out o' seet,
  Seafe frae this canker'd she,
I pray and pray wi' aw my heart,
  Death, suin tek her or me !
Flyte, flytin' !—feight, feightin' !
  How her luik I dree !
Come tyrant rid me o' this curse,
  Dui tek her !—I'll thank thee !

THE LASSES OF CAREL.

The lasses o' Carel are weel-shep'd and bonny,
  But he that wad win yen mun brag of his gear ;
You may follow, and follow, till heart-sick and weary,
  To git them needs siller, and fine claes to wear :
They'll catch at a reed cwoat, like as monie mack'rel,
  And jump at a fop, or e'en lissen a fuil ;
Just brag of an uncle that's got heaps of money,
  And deil a bit odds, if you've ne'er been at schuil !

I yence follow'd Marget, the toast amang aw maks,
  And Peg hed a reed cheek, and bonny dark e'e ;
But suin as she fan' I depended on labour,
  She snurl'd up her neb, and nae mair luik'd at me

This meks my words gud, nobbet brag o' yer uncle,
　And git a peer hawf-wit to trumpet your praise,
You may catch whee you will, they'll caress ye, and
　　bless ye—
　It's money, nit merit, they seek now-a-days !

I neist follow'd Nelly, and thowt her an angel,
　And she thowt me aw that a mortal sud be :
A rich whupper-snapper just stept in atween us,
　Nae words efter that pass'd atween Nell and me :
This meks my words gud, nobbet brag o' yer uncle,
　They'll feight, ay like mad cats, to win yer sly
　　smile ;
And watch ye, to catch ye, now gazin' and praisin',
　They're angels to luik at, wi' hearts full o' guile !

WILLIAM WORDSWORTH,

BORN AT COCKERMOUTH 1770:
DIED AT RYDAL MOUNT 1850.

"Sole king of rocky Cumberland."

LUCY GRAY.

[When Mr. Wordsworth and I were on that noble spot, the amphitheatre at Nismes, I observed his eyes fixed in a direction where there was little to be seen ; and looking that way I beheld two very young children at play with flowers, and overheard him saying to himself, "O you darlings, I wish I could put you in my pocket and carry you to Rydal Mount!"—*Recollections of a Tour in Italy by Henry Crabb Robinson.*]

FT I had heard of Lucy Gray :
And, when I crossed the wild,
I chanced to see at break of day
The solitary child.

No mate, no comrade Lucy knew ;
She dwelt on a wide moor,
—The sweetest thing that ever grew
Beside a human door !

You yet may spy the fawn at play,
The hare upon the green ;
But the sweet face of Lucy Gray
Will never more be seen.

" To-night will be a stormy night—
You to the town must go ;
And take a lantern, Child, to light
Your mother through the snow."

" That, Father ! will I gladly do :
'Tis scarcely afternoon—
The minster-clock has just struck two,
And yonder is the moon !"

At this the Father raised his hook,
And snapped a faggot-band ;
He plied his work ;—and Lucy took
The lantern in her hand.

Not blither is the mountain roe :
With many a wanton stroke
Her feet disperse the powdery snow,
That rises up like smoke.

The storm came on before its time :
She wandered up and down ;
And many a hill did Lucy climb :
But never reached the town.

The wretched parents all that night
Went shouting far and wide ;
But there was neither sound nor sight
To serve them for a guide.

At day-break on a hill they stood
That overlooked the moor ;
And thence they saw the bridge of wood,
A furlong from their door.

They wept—and, turning homeward, cried,
" In heaven we all shall meet ;"
—When in the snow the mother spied
The print of Lucy's feet.

Then downwards from the steep hill's edge
They tracked the footmarks small ;
And through the broken hawthorn hedge,
And by the long stone-wall ;

And then an open field they crossed :
The marks were still the same ;
They tracked them on, nor ever lost ;
And to the bridge they came.

They followed from the snowy bank
Those footmarks, one by one,
Into the middle of the plank ;
And further there were none !

—Yet some maintain that to this day
She is a living child ;
That you may see sweet Lucy Gray
Upon the lonesome wild.

O'er rough and smooth she trips along.
And never looks behind ;
And sings a solitary song
That whistles in the wind.

THE PET-LAMB.

[Barbara Lewthwaite, now residing at Ambleside (1843),
though much changed as to beauty, was one of two most lovely
sisters.   Almost the first words my poor brother John said,
when he visited us at Grasmere, were, "Were those two
angels that I have just seen?" and from his description I have
no doubt they were those two sisters.   The mother died in
childbed ; and one of our neighbours, at Grasmere, told me
that the loveliest sight she had ever seen was that mother as
she lay in her coffin with her dead babe in her arm.   I men-
tion this to notice what I cannot but think a salutary custom,
once universal in these vales : every attendant on a funeral
made it a duty to look at the corpse in the coffin before the
lid was closed, which was never done (nor I believe is now)
till a minute or two before the corpse was removed.   Barbara
Lewthwaite was not, in fact, the child whom I had seen and
overheard as engaged in the poem.   I chose the name for
reasons implied in the above, and will here add a caution
against the use of names of living persons.   Within a few
months after the publication of this poem, I was much sur-
prised, and more hurt, to find it in a child's school book,
which, having been compiled by Lindley Murray, had come
into use at Grasmere school, where Barbara was a pupil.
And, alas, I had the mortification of hearing that she was
very vain of being thus distinguished ; and, in after life, she
used to say that she remembered the incident, and what I said
to her upon the occasion.—NOTE BY WORDSWORTH.]

The dew was falling fast, the stars began to blink ;
I heard a voice; it said, " Drink, pretty creature,
    drink !"
And, looking o'er the hedge, before me I espied
A snow-white mountain-lamb with a Maiden at its
    side.

Nor sheep nor kine were near ; the lamb was all
    alone,
And by a slender cord was tethered to a stone ;
With one knee on the grass did the little Maiden
    kneel,   .
While to that mountain-lamb she gave its evening
    meal.

The lamb, while from her hand he thus his supper
    took,
Seemed to feast with head and ears ; and his tail
    with pleasure shook.
" Drink, pretty creature, drink," she said in such a
    tone
That I almost received her heart into my own.

'Twas little Barbara Lewthwaite, a child of beauty
    rare !
I watched them with delight they were a lovely pair.
Now with her empty can the Maiden turned away :
But ere ten yards were gone her footsteps did she
    stay.

Right towards the lamb she looked; and from a
shady place
I unobserved could see the workings of her face :
If Nature to her tongue could measured numbers
bring,
Thus, thought I, to her lamb that little Maid might
sing:

" What ails thee, young One? what? Why pull so
at thy cord?
Is it not well with thee? well both for bed and board?
Thy plot of grass is soft, and green as grass can be ;
Rest, little young One, rest ; what is 't that aileth
thee?

What is it thou wouldst seek? What is wanting to
thy heart?
Thy limbs are they not strong? And beautiful thou
art :
This grass is tender grass ; these flowers they have
no peers ;
And that green corn all day is rustling in thy ears !

If the sun be shining hot, do but stretch thy woollen
chain,
This beech is standing by, its covert thou canst
gain ;

For rain and mountain-storms ! the like thou need'st
    not fear,
The rain and storm are things that scarcely can
    come here.

Rest, little young One, rest ; thou hast forgot the
    day
When my father found thee first in places far away ;
Many flocks were on the hills, but thou wert owned
    by none,
And thy mother from thy side for evermore was
    gone.

He took thee in his arms, and in pity brought thee
    home :
A blessed day for thee ! then whither wouldst thou
    roam ?
A faithful nurse thou hast ; the dam that did thee
    yean
Upon the mountain tops no kinder could have been.

Thou know'st that twice a day I have brought thee
    in this can
Fresh water from the brook, as clear as ever ran ;
And twice in the day, when the ground is wet with
    dew,
I bring thee draughts of milk, warm milk it is and
    new.

Thy limbs will shortly be twice as stout as they are
    now,
Then I'll yoke thee to my cart like a pony in the
    plough ;
My playmate thou shalt be : and when the wind is
    cold
Our hearth shall be thy bed, our house shall be thy
    fold.

It will not, will not rest !—Poor creature, can it be
That 'tis thy mother's heart which is working so in
    thee ?
Things that I know not of belike to thee are dear,
And dreams of things which thou canst neither see
    nor hear.

Alas, the mountain-tops that look so green and fair !
I've heard of fearful winds and darkness that come
    there ;
The little brooks that seem all pastime and all play,
When they are angry, roar like lions for their prey.

Here thou need'st not dread the raven in the sky ;
          thou art safe,—our cottage is hard by.
Why bleat so after me ?   Why pull so at thy chain ?
Sleep—and at break of day I will come to thee
    again !"

—As homeward through the lane I went with lazy
 feet,
This song to myself did I oftentimes repeat ;
And it seemed, as I retraced the ballad line by line,
That but half of it was hers, and one half of it was
 mine.

Again, and once again, did I repeat the song ;
" Nay," said I, " more than half to the damsel must
 belong,
For she looked with such a look, and she spake with
 such a tone,
That I almost received her heart into my own."

1800.

MATTHEW.

[This piece, with several kindred ones, are supposed to refer
to one of Wordsworth's masters, "a blithe man, with hair of
glittering grey," at the Hawkshead grammar school. The
joys of the great poet's school-day life seem never to have
departed from his memory ; and it is said that when travelling
among the most sublime scenery on the continent, his mind
was often roaming among his youthful haunts on the banks of
Esthwaite lake and Windermere.]

We talked with open heart, and tongue
Affectionate and true,
A pair of friends, though I was young,   .
And Matthew seventy-two.

We lay beneath a spreading oak,
Beside a mossy seat;
And from the turf a fountain broke,
And gurgled at our feet.

"Now, Matthew!" said I, "let us match
This water's pleasant tune
With some old border-song, or catch
That suits a summer's noon;

Or of the church-clock and the chimes
Sing here beneath the shade,
That half-mad thing of witty rhymes
Which you last April made!"

In silence Matthew lay, and eyed
The spring beneath the tree;
And thus the dear old Man replied,
The grey-haired man of glee:

"No check, no stay, this Streamlet fears;
How merrily it goes!
'Twill murmur on a thousand years,
And flow as now it flows.

And here, on this delightful day,
I cannot chose but think
How oft, a vigorous man, I lay
Beside this fountain's brink.

My eyes are dim with childish tears,
My heart is idly stirred,
For the same sound is in my ears
Which in those days I heard.

Thus fares it still in our decay :
And yet the wiser mind
Mourns less for what age takes away
Than what it leaves behind.

The blackbird amid leafy trees,
The lark above the hill,
Let loose their carols when they please,
Are quiet when they will.

With Nature never do *they* wage
A foolish strife ; they see
A happy youth, and their old age
Is beautiful and free :

But we are pressed by heavy laws ;
And often, glad no more,
We wear a face of joy, because
We have been glad of yore.

If there be one who need bemoan
His kindred laid in earth,
The household hearts that were his own ;
It is the man of mirth.

My days, my Friend, are almost gone,
My life has been approved,
And many love me ; but by none
Am I enough beloved."

" Now both himself and me he wrongs,
The man who thus complains !
I live and sing my idle songs
Upon these happy plains ;

And, Matthew, for thy children dead
I'll be a son to thee !"
At this he grasped my hand, and said,
" Alas ! that cannot be."

We rose up from the fountain-side ;
And down the smooth descent
Of the green sheep-track did we glide ;
And through the wood we went ;

And, ere we came to Leonard's rock,
He sang those witty rhymes
About the crazy old church-clock,
And the bewildered chimes.

1799.

THE CUCKOO.

[There is an anecdote told of a poor crazed woman who lived near Rydal, which shows in a striking manner the habits of the great poet. This woman was once asked if she knew Wordsworth, and what sort of a man he was. "Oh, indeed," said she, "he's canny enuff at times ; an' tho' he gaes *booing his pottery* thro' the woods, he'll noo an' than say, ' Hoo d'ye do, Nanny ?' as sensible as ye or me !"]

O blithe New-comer ! I have heard,
I hear thee and rejoice.
O Cuckoo ! shall I call thee Bird,
Or but a wandering voice ?

While I am lying on the grass
Thy twofold shout I hear,
From hill to hill it seems to pass,
At once far off, and near.

Though babbling only to the Vale,
Of sunshine and of flowers,
Thou bringest unto me a tale
Of visionary hours.

Thrice welcome, darling of the Spring !
Even yet thou art to me
No bird, but an invisible thing,
A voice, a mystery ;

The same whom in my school-boy days
I listened to ; that Cry
Which made me look a thousand ways
In bush, and tree, and sky.

To seek thee did I often rove
Through woods and on the green ;
And thou wert still a hope, a love ;
Still longed for, never seen.

And I can listen to thee yet ;
Can lie upon the plain
And listen, till I do beget
That golden time again.

O blessed Bird ! the earth we pace
Again appears to be
An unsubstantial, faery place ;
That is fit home for Thee !

THE COCK IS CROWING.

[This little lyrical piece was a great favorite with Joanna
Baillie. In Miss Wordsworth's Diary, the circumstances
under which it was composed are thus described :—" When
we came to the foot of *Brother's Water*, left William sitting
on the Bridge. I went along the path on the right side of the
lake, delighted with what I saw : the bare old trees, the
simplicity of the mountains, and the exquisite beauty of the
path. . . When I returned, found William writing
a poem descriptive of the sights and sounds we saw and heard.
There was the gentle flow of the stream, the glittering lake, a
flat pasture with forty-two cattle feeding ; to our left, the road
leading to the hamlet ; no smoke there, the sun shining on the
bare roofs : the people at work, ploughing, harrowing, sowing ;
cocks crowing, birds twittering ; the snow in patches at the
top of the highest hills. William finished his verses before we
got to the foot of Kirkstone."]

The cock is crowing,
The stream is flowing,
The small birds twitter,
The lake doth glitter,
The green fields sleep in the sun ;
The oldest and youngest
Are at work with the strongest ;
The cattle are grazing,
Their heads never raising ;
There are forty feeding like one !

Like an army defeated
The snow hath retreated,
And now doth fare ill
On the top of the bare hill ;
The Ploughboy is whooping—anon—anon ;
There's joy in the mountains ;
There's life in the fountains ;
Small clouds are sailing,
Blue sky prevailing,
The rain is over and gone !

JOHN RAYSON.

OHN RAYSON was for many years the sole survivor of those writers who, commencing with Relph, have swelled the poetical literature of Cumberland to so considerable a volume. On the father's side he was descended from a family which has been settled at Aglionby, near Carlisle, from time immemorial. The name is found in the Court Rolls spelled as Raison, Raeson, &c., and the probability is that the family has lived at Aglionby since the Norman conquest. The early part of Rayson's life was spent on his father's estate, but the intention seems to have been to make him a draper. He was in business at Carlisle, and also in London, and in both instances failed. For some time, too, he filled the situation of attorney's clerk, at Penrith, but did not relish the drudgery of such employment. Undoubtedly the kind of life best suited to his own temperament was that of village schoolmaster, and to this occupation he devoted himself for many years of his life, teaching in various parts of Cumberland with more or less success. In the free and easy style of living followed by the schoolmasters of the last generation, Rayson was quite at home. He was a favourite with the farmers, writing their letters, and making their wills, and received as the principal part of his remuneration free " whittlegate," as customary at that time. In 1845 he obtained the appointment of assistant overseer to the Penrith Union, and became a very efficient parish officer. But having got embarassed in his circumstances he was obliged to resign this situation, which, no doubt, preyed upon his mind, and perhaps shortened his existence. He died of disease of the heart, September 12th, 1859, aged fifty-six years, and was buried in Warwick churchyard.

Rayson commenced as a rhymester about the time that Robert Anderson was in the zenith of his fame, and it must be added, in the lowest deep of depression and neglect. Whilst Anderson, in despair, was about "to commit his unpublished pieces to the flames" (1824), Rayson made his first appearance in the columns of the *Citizen*, a fortnightly periodical then issuing in Carlisle, with "Lines on the Cumberland Bard," written for the purpose of bringing aid to the elder poet. Rather poor encouragement for poets !—nevertheless, Rayson continued a contributor to the *Citizen* while it lasted, and subsequently to other local prints. Several years ago he published a small volume of his ballads, but it was not until 1858 that he was enabled to bring

II. 14

out a complete edition to include his latest and best pieces. Prince Louis Lucien Buonaparte employed him to vernacularise the Song of Solomon, to form part of a large work on languages and dialects ; and to him Rayson inscribed his poems.

Of the merits of Rayson's productions we can only speak comparatively ; as the best of Anderson's ballads come near the general level of Burns's effusions, so are the best of Rayson's up to the average of Anderson's. In them we get a slight insight into the fast-changing manners of Cumberland, but in this respect Anderson is an undoubted superior to the other Cumbrian writers. The greater part of Rayson's ballads are of course written on the "lasses," and of heroines there is an abundance ; but we cannot discover much variety in the delineation, or individuality in the characters. Certain it is, however, that with Rayson, as with many other writers, where his feelings are enlisted the poetical inspiration is most manifest. The *Auld Pauper*, the *Tom Cat*, etc., are favourable instances of this class.

THE AULD PAUPER.

E'RE auld and feeble now, Jean,
Our days will not be lang ;
They've telt me at the Board, Jean,
To workhouse we mun gang ;
My heart was lyke to break, Jean,
But them I cou'd not bleame,
They said it was not law, Jean,
To give us bread at heame.

We've toil'd togidder lang, Jean,
Content wi' frugal fare ;
'Tis hard to part us now, Jean,
When we can work nae mair :
We'll for our few days left, Jean,
Be frae each other torn ;
I hop'd we would hae died, Jean,
In peace where we were born.

'Twas hard when our three sons, Jean,
Aw nearly up to men,
And fit to dui us gud, Jean,
Death summon'd yen by yen :

And that sweet lass in Heaven, Jean,
Wha taught us how to pray—
At neet I hear her voice, Jean,
Oft calling us away.

We'll hae nae mair a heame, Jean,
Till we're amang the blest,
Where wicked cease oppressing,
" And weary are at rest ;"
Sae dry thy falling tears, Jean,
It gives my bosom pain,
We'll meet where cruel laws, Jean,
Will ne'er part us ageane.

ANN O' HETHERSGILL.

The fairest maids o' Britain's isle
'Mang Cumbria's mountains dwell ;
Sweet budding flowers unseen they bloom
By muirland, glen, or fell.
An' yen, the fairest o' them aw,
My heart cou'd ne'er be still,
To see her at the kurk or fair,
Sweet Ann o' Hethersgill.

Her feace was like the blushing rose,
Her heart was leet and free,
Ere she had felt the world's cares,
Or love blink'd in her e'e.

This fair bewitching feace wi' love
The hardest heart wad fill ;
The flower o' aw the country side
Was Ann o' Hethersgill.

She cheerful wrought her war-day work,
Then sat down at her wheel,
And sang o' luive the winter's neets,
Ere she its pow'r did feel :
And at the kurk, on Sunday mworns,
Nane sang sae sweet and shrill ;
The charming voice abuin them aw
Was Ann's o' Hethersgill.

But she saw Jock at Carel fair,—
She nae mair was hersel ;
She cudna sing when at her wheel,
And sigh'd oft down the dell.
Jock is the laird o' Souter Muir,—
He's now come o'er the hill,
And teane away his bonny bride,
Sweet Ann o' Hethersgill.

THE TOM CAT.

[Tom, the subject of the following ballad, was brought up by the author at his office in Penrith. "He was," says the *Kendal Mercury*, "decidedly a prince amongst cats, and no cat ought to have been more proud of his position. Unfortunately, however, he had a great predilection for a vagabond life. He left his comfortable home on the Beacon-side for the wild woods, where he lived for months together: and though he occasionally returned to see his old master, and made sundry promises of reformation, yet he ultimately became one of the most abandoned cats in the country."]

Thou's wander'd frae thy heame, Tom,
Past thy accustom'd roun's,
And left thy own grimalkins here
For cats o' other towns ;
Thou'lt be, nae doubt, ere lang, Tom,
Catch'd in the poacher's snare,
Or kill'd wi' dogs and guns, Tom,
Then we'll see thee nae mair.

Thy milk's ay set for thee, Tom,
And hes been aw the week ;
The mice now, as they run, Tom,
In ivery corner, squeak :
They care not for the kitten, Tom,
That play'd wi' thee at neet ;
It often mews for thee, Tom,
And makes yen wae to see't.

It luiks oft in the garden, Tom,
Where thou wast last time seen,
And runs aw roun' about the house
Where thou and it hev been.
It hes nae cat to play wi' now,
To chase it round the room ;
It will not jump at ribbons now,
But sits in silent gloom.

Thou'd lal to do but eat, Tom,
And lie in cushan'd chair ;
Thou kens not when thou's weel, Tom,
Thou's ower like monie mair—
Just like the houseless wanderer
Who happy might hae been,
But ranks amang the vagabonds,
The meanest o' the mean.

When thou is far frae heame, Tom,
Thou'll miss auld Crummy's milk,
Which meade thee fat and fair, Tom,
Wi' skin like ony silk.
Sir Jeamie's* naval store, Tom,
Avoid wi' aw thy care,
The bastile o' the cats, Tom,
Or milk thou'll teaste nae mair.

---

* It was reported, that Sir James Graham, when Lord of
the Admirality, stopped the usual supply of milk to the cats
kept in the naval store.

I've little hopes left now, Tom.
That iver thou wilt mend,
But I would be content, Tom,
If I could know thy end.
How wilt thou feace thy mistress, Tom?
With her, black is thy neame;
Content be, like thy master, Tom,
Wi' some cat nearer heame.

I try thee to excuse, Tom,
To reet and wrang thou's blind,
Yet thou but plays a like part
Wi' brutes o' human kind.
When human bodies err, Tom,
We cannot thee condemn;
Thou seems a harmless brute, Tom,
Compar'd to sec as them.

When e'er I stray frae heame, Tom,
Past my appointed time,
Whiles musing in the wood, Tom,
In " blethering up a rhyme,"
I oft git hints o' thee, Tom,
In wandering away—
Come heame, and we'll reform, Tom,
And gang nae mair astray.

CHARLIE M'GLEN.

Lal Charlie M'Glen, he was brong up a pedder,
A wutless bit hav'ril, a conceited yape ;
He selt beggar-inkle, caps, muslins, and cottons,
Goons, neck'loths, and stockings, thread, needles,
   and tape.
'Tis whuspert by sleet-han' he's meade lots o' money ;
His actions now pruive him the weale o' bad men :
He's guilty o' crimes that desarve him a gallows—
For biggest o' rascals is Charlie M'Glen.

Puir Bella, the wife, she's a decent man's douter,
And prays oft that Heaven wad give her relief ;
She's e'en been bedevel'd, like meast o' young lasses,
And claims to our pity, she's join'd till a thief.
A reace, fair, or market, he seldom yen misses—
The Carel street-robbers he kens monie yen ;
For burds of a feather they ay flock togidder,
And sae mun thur villians wi' Charlie M'Glen.

At Skinburness reaces he pick'd a man's pocket—
For slape-finger'd art he is equall'd by neane ;
But he was o'erseen, and they seiz'd the vile sharper,
And fworc'd him to give back the money ageane.
At Abbey, last week, he fell in wi' Kit Stewart,
And crowns frae his pocket he gat nine or ten ;
But suin for that job he was teane by the beaylics,
But money frae prison seav'd Charlic M'Glen.

He's seldom at heame, and his wife's kept in terror,—
At neets i' the lonnings he's seen at aw times ;
A swindlin' rascal he's been frae his cradle,—
It's nit in yen's power to outnumber his crimes ;
For he steals hens and ducks wi' thur neet-strolling
      fellows,
Oh ! happy's the country that's clear o' sec men !
I whope that my lword, at the next Carel 'sizes,
Will ship o'er the herring-dub Charlie M'Glen.

LINES

ADDRESSED TO A ROBIN WHICH THE AUTHOR FED ON
HIS GARDEN WALL DURING THE WINTER.

What, Robin, wilt thou leave me now ?
    The wintry storms are past—
The snow from off the mountain's brow
    Is disappearing fast :
Again there's music in the wood,
    Thy mate's on yonder tree ;
The lark and thrush in concert join
    In sweetest harmony.

Seek some retreat to build thy nest
    In woodside bowers among,
And cease thy doleful winter chirp,
    And tune thy summer song ;

John Rayson.

And when I walk at evening's hour
    Along the shady lane,
I'll hear thee in the hawthorn bush
    Pour forth thy plaintive strain.

So, Robin, go and leave me now,
    I never can thee blame,
When all to me of humankind
    Have ever done the same.
Pretending friends I us'd the best
    Who on my bounty fed,
When once I felt adversity
    I found they all had fled.

It matter'd not whate'er they were,
    False friends or open foes,
They basely all combin'd to add
    Fresh burthens to my woes :
They stole my purse and left me poor,
    And now in life's decline ;
They take from me what's dearer still,
    " Good name" and peace of mind.

But, Robin, thou'rt "not man but bird"
    From which we never find
Such proofs of base ingratitude
    As shown by human kind :
So join the vocal throng, and pass
    The summer months away ;
I know thou'lt sometimes come at eve
    And sing thy grateful lay.

And when the wintry blasts return,
And ice-bound is the rill,
Come to my garden wall again,
And thou shalt have thy fill ;
And through the storms of frost and snow,
My plain and humble fare,
Both thee and thy red-breasted mates
Are welcome still to share.

MISCELLANEOUS SONGS.

VULCAN'S CAVE.

[This fragment is by MARK LONSDALE, the author of the
Upshot, the *Old Commodore*, &c. The burden, *Twank-a-
dillo, &c.*, with the music, was sent to the editor by JOHN
WOODCOCK GRAVES, of Hobart Town, Tasmania.]

HUS we work, like jovial fellows,
Drink and sing and blow the bellows,
When hissing sparks around us fly,
And lips are parch'd and throats are dry,
Then, then's the time to wet your eye,
And blow, blow the bellows.—(Blows)—
" *Twank-a-dillo, twank-a-dillo,*
Twank-a-dillo—dillo—dillo ;
And we play'd our merry pipes
Down by the green willow.

THE LUCK OF EDENHALL.

From Walter White's "Northumberland and the Border."

[A crystal spring bubbles up into a small square stone basin, and flows away in a perennial stream along a channel in the smooth green turf. Here, according to tradition, the fairies were dancing and drinking one night when the butler came to draw water, they started in alarm and prepared to fly; but having dropped their crystal beaker the man picked it up, and turning a deaf ear to the entreaties of the fays for restoration of their treasure, he brought it to his master, hearing plaintive voices say as he turned away,

"If that cup shall break or fall,
Farewell the Luck of Edenhall."]

'Twas summer-tide, when days are long,
　And holm and haugh are green ;
And the mavis sings in the good greenwood,
　And chatters the jay between.

"O, whither dost run thou little foot-page,
　As swift as hawk on wing?"
"For life—for life, to Penrith town
　I run the leech to bring!"

"And wherefore seekest thou the leech?
　Now up, and tell to me."
"O, hold me not thou weird woman,
　There's glamour in thine ee!"

Oh, there was glamour in her ee;
　He could not choose but tell:
"My mistress lieth in deadly swoon,—
　The lady Isabel."

" Now run, now run, thou little foot-page,
   Run swift as hawk on wing ;
But if the leech to succour fail,
   Then seek the fairies' spring."

The little foot-page hath gone and come,
   So nimble of foot was he ;
And his bonnie bright een were wet with tears,
   For he loved his dear ladye.

The leech he rode to Edenhall,
   The while uprose the moon :
But his craft was vain, and his simples naught,
   To loose the deadly swoon.

The little foot-page, he wept full sore,
   And he fell on his knee and he prayed :
He prayed a prayer to Mary Mother,
   And Saint Cuthbert to aid.

His dear ladye hath nurtured him
   Since rose his infant wail,
That night his father's hut was burnt
   By thieves from Liddesdale.

Then thought he of that weird woman,
   But, oh ! 'tis a fearsome thing
To go at night, in the wan moonlight,
   And walk by the fairies' spring.

Yet will he forth, whate'er betide,
 Yet will he forth and see ;
For who loveth he on earth beside,
 If not his dear ladye ?

So softly crept he down the stair,
 And out by the secret door ;
And he was aware of a strange music
 He never had heard before.

And slowly paced he o'er the mead,
 And heard the self-same sound ;
And there he saw a companye
 A-dancing round and round.

He fell on his knee behind a bush,
 And his heart beat quick for fear,
Whenever he saw the dainty folk
 Come dancing him a-near.

So beautiful their faces shone,
 So bright their silken sheen ;
He could but dread to look thereon,
 And yet he looked, I ween.

Oh, merrily did they laugh and dance,
 Still tripping round and round ;
But not a blade of grass did bend,
 No flower sunk on the ground.

And ever the music rang full sweet,
  Yet sat no players there ;
It was as if the trees did sing,
  While tinkled harps in air.

Anon they pause, and a crystal cup
  Is dipped in the bubbling spring,
And gliding goes, from lip to lip,
  All round the fairy ring.

And ever it dips and fills again,
  And while the revellers drink
The brimming water falls like pearls
  Down from the sparkling brink.

But the fay that bears that cup around
  No mortal eye may see.
"Oh, could my ladye drain that cup !"
  Thought the little foot-page on knee.

Scarce had he thought than to him glides
  The cup from the bubbling spring ;
Him paused before, yet who it bore
  Did nought of shadow fling.

He trembled sore, but he took the cup,
  For the sake of his dear ladye :
And fast the drops fell down like pearls
  As he rose up from knee.

And at his feet, upon the grass,
    A written scroll was thrown ;
Then all at once the music ceased,
    And the fairy folk were gone.

He took the scroll, and he took the cup,
    Them to the hall he bore ;
The Lady Isabel did drink,
    And her deadly swoon was o'er.

And the little foot-page he brought the scroll,
    And showed it to his lord ;
Sir Ralph he looked thereon and read,
    In olden style the word—

        " Jf that cuppe
            Shal breake or falle,
        Farewel the Lucke
            Of Edenhalle."

Sir Ralph de Musgrave made a feast,
    For joy over his ladye ;
And the little foot-page he stood by her chair,
    And blithest of all was he.

Sir Ralph de Musgrave built a church,
    In sweet St. Cuthbert's prayse,
That men might know whence came the Lucke.
    And think thereon alwayes.

G. AND T. COWARD, PRINTERS, CARLISLE.